# SMALL HOMES

Interior Details

AN IMPRINT OF

PBC INTERNATIONAL, INC.

DESIGNING FOR

# SMALL HOMES

DYLAN LANDIS

*Distributor to the book trade in the United States and Canada*
Rizzoli International Publications
through St. Martin's Press
175 Fifth Avenue
New York, NY 10010

*Distributor to the art trade in the United States and Canada*
PBC International, Inc.
One School Street
Glen Cove, NY 11542

*Distributor throughout the rest of the world*
Hearst Books International
1350 Avenue of the Americas
New York, NY 10019

Library of Congress Cataloging–in–Publication Data

Landis, Dylan, 1956–
    Designing for small homes / Dylan Landis
        p.   cm.
    Includes index.
    ISBN 0-86636-378-5 (hardcover)   (pb 0-86636-440-4)
    1. Interior decoration—Human factors.  2. Room layout (Dwellings).
    3. Personal space—Psychological aspects.  I.  Title.
NK2113.L36  1996                        96–4914
728—dc20                                CIP

Credits
page 10    From "The Long… And Short of It; All the World
                in One Room," by William L. Hamilton. Copyright ©1995
                by The New York Times Company. Reprinted by permission.

CAVEAT– Information in this text is believed accurate, and will pose no
problem for the student or casual reader.  However, the author was often
constrained by information contained in signed release forms, information
that could have been in error or not included at all.  Any misinformation
(or lack of information) is the result of failure in these attestations.  The
author has done whatever is possible to insure accuracy.

Designed by Garrett Schuh

Color separation by Fine Arts Repro House Co., Ltd., Hong Kong
Printing and binding by C&C Joint Printing Co., (H.K.) Ltd., Hong Kong

10 9 8 7 6 5 4 3 2

Printed in Hong Kong

To my parents, Erica and Bern Landis

"It's not the size of the space that makes it exciting, but the feeling of wanting to be drawn through the rooms." *~ Carl D'Aquino*

# contents

# FOREWORD

When America's top fashion designers turn their talents to home furnishings, and shops from Madison Avenue in New York to King's Road in London suddenly sport more sofas than shoes, even *The Wall Street Journal* notices that something's afoot. The Friday edition of that venerable

paper now runs a "home page," a phrase common to anyone who surfs the Internet: It refers to the starting point for a Web site, and conjures an image, of course, of a safe place, a home base, a desirable destination — which is just what we in the design business have *always* meant when we talked about home.

Even the Yankelovich Monitor, a keystone marketing study, tells us that consumers ranked redecorating their homes as their third-highest goal to achieve — behind having more fun and losing weight, but well out in front of travel, saving money and a number of other enticing options.

Interest in home has rarely been more profound. In the '80s, designer labels were practically required, and big, expensively furnished houses were part of the success image. But the new realities of the '90s have taught us again to value our inner feelings above the awed reactions of our peers. Our personal spaces have evolved from showplaces to comfortable retreats that express our personalities and suit our individual lifestyles. Many of these sanctuaries aren't the large castles we dreamed of as children, but apartments, condos or cottages that are far more convenient, practical and stress-free.

Faced with a small room — or a small house — many people just give up on the notion of style. They paint everything white and do a minimal furnishings job using only Lilliputian-sized pieces, achieving a livable look that doesn't thrill because it neither reveals nor risks.

Dylan Landis's stunning book celebrates hundreds of imaginative options. There's a tremendous style range to be found here: ubiquitous '50s "white boxes," as we call them, as well as Arts and Crafts cottages, tiny bungalows, vernacular guest houses, log cabins, lodges and urban studios. The smallest is 440 square feet; the largest 1,200. Some solutions are the expected ones, but they are exceptionally well executed: glass doors and mirrored surfaces, built-ins, outdoor spaces that extend the indoors. But many are delightful surprises: games of scale (you *don't* have to use

small scale furniture in a small room — often one large piece, or more, will trick the eye); floor treatments; "space widening" fabrics on both upholstery and walls; color that goes from light to shadow; skirted tables with secret storage behind the pleats and folds.

This is, in fact, a book for everyone who loves their home by a writer known across the industry for her insight and fine writing as well as her love of home. It's the perfect volume for anyone who is looking for inspiration and ideas to make their home work harder and live easier — whether it's small or large.

**DONNA WARNER**, Editor in Chief
*Metropolitan Home*

# INTRODUCTION  *Dylan Landis*

A compact home, once you stop fighting the boundaries, is really about comfort, intimacy, and living with the essentials.

A diminutive room with red walls can feel like a jewel. A cottage with nooks and engaging vignettes will invite, and reward, exploration. In a small home, possessions are distilled to the beautiful and the necessary, and everything you need is within reach. "The pillow for the head finds a wall more conveniently," wrote William L. Hamilton in a *New York Times* essay. "The book will not fall far when you sleep."

The 38 houses and apartments that follow, each by an interior designer or architect, are proof that you don't need to live in a ballroom to live well. "I *like* the scale of small rooms," says Carl D'Aquino, who has three of them, tall and sunlit, in his own 700-square-foot apartment. When the proportions are right, he explains, a small space becomes a restful embrace, putting people at ease.

It's also true that a vest-pocket dwelling may represent, for its owner, a tough compromise. Perhaps square footage was traded for a river view, or sacrificed for the wherewithal to live in Paris

or New York. But when the place is intelligently designed — when storage is resourceful, and rooms can adapt to more than one use — the interior *works*, often better than a residence twice its size.

The habitats in this book have been redesigned and customized to fit their owners' needs. Witness the New York penthouse by Clodagh: At 9:00 A.M. it opens as an elegant office from which a national business is run. At night the workspaces retract into their cabinetry and, for all practical purposes, vanish, leaving a startled visitor to marvel at what has suddenly become a sumptuous rooftop retreat.

Sometimes, the solutions start with architecture. Rooms get merged, doorways widened, shelves built in, and storage slotted into every unused corner. Tray ceilings are scooped out, or French doors

installed. No matter how recalcitrant an interior seems, it usually can be carved into something airier and more serviceable. Consider the ingenuity of an Italian architect, forced to squeeze guest quarters into an impossibly small home: He raised a section of the floor and slid low, twin beds beneath it.

As for fabrics, furnishings and paint, they often make up brilliantly for structural sins. Most strategies fall somewhere near one of two camps:

*The pry-it-open-with-white approach*. Some designers expand rooms by expressing the backdrop, and key furnishings, in a hundred shades of pale. Boundaries, less intrusive, seem to drop out of conscious awareness. But notice the ingredients: They are textured, luxurious, sensual — anything but bland. Sandra Nunnerley, teasing open her own one-bedroom apartment, has stirred in silk moire, Parisian fringe, linen, leather and wood, all in various hues of white. Those subtle contrasts sustain your interest, while river views enlarge the space.

*The saturate-it-with-color approach*. When a small interior offers a mix of experiences, it can take on the spirit of a larger home. D'Aquino applied this principle in an artist's narrow town house, painting rooms in different colors until they were as vivid, and as varied, as the artworks on the walls. Now, meandering from pumpkin living room to cobalt dining room, a visitor subconsciously assumes that the house must be extensive — how else could it offer such divergent moods?

Both tactics work. And both can be carried out in personal, evocative ways. Only one factor is completely shared by all of these interiors: the designers' conviction that even the smallest home can be visually expansive, supremely functional, and worthy of celebration.

"Most small spaces are too simple. Complexity, especially architectural complexity, is quite a luxury." ~ *David Weingarten*

*houses*

## DIANE THOMPSON & GOODMAN CHARLTON

## On a Grand Scale
### Los Angeles, California

1,100 square feet/102.19 square meters

This low-profile Hollywood bungalow started out with five small rooms and two saving graces: banks of built-in cabinetry, original to the 1920s architecture — and a design team that knew how to pry open tight spaces without budging a single wall.

Interior designer Diane Thompson, a partner in the avant-garde furniture store Modern Living, owns the house; her collaborators were Jeffrey Goodman and Steven Charlton, whose voluptuous furnishings she sells. To elevate the unpretentious bungalow, they agreed, scale would be the critical design element. They began with the floor, painting yard-long white diamonds across the oak planks, inviting the eye to sweep across the space. "It implies a much bigger house," says Thompson.

Strong colors on the walls, rather than diminishing the rooms, work to enlarge them. The home office adds up to merely 120 square feet, for example, yet its fir-colored paint vests it with the authority of an English library. "The boundaries of a room get lost in a dark color," says Goodman. As for white, it was applied largely to heighten ceilings and for a crisp effect on moldings and paneling.

Goodman Charlton's own seating is upholstered in velvet and damask, evoking images of grander rooms; and each piece is deliberately oversized. Explains Goodman: "It contributes a boldness, and in effect a largeness, to an otherwise diminutive house."

**Above**  *The trellised porch adds a tiny outdoor chamber, almost a sixth room, at the entry. Strong, primary colors in the garden reiterate the paint colors inside.*

*Photography by Dominique Vorillon*

**Opposite**  *Philippe Starck's narrow M table seats eight in the dining room while allowing easy passage on both sides to the French doors and garden beyond. The Doge side chairs, with their white canvas slipcovers, are by Goodman Charlton.*

**Opposite**  *Kitchen walls were glazed  in ocher and siena, old-world Tuscan shades that complement the Italian crockery and new Italian cooking utensils. A weathered hutch was notched into one corner for added storage, while a farm table, its rough yellow paint added by the designers, works as counterspace or breakfast spot.*

**Above**  *Diane Thompson designed the floor-to-ceiling mahogany workstation for the home office, then added a shot of steel with the Dolphin chair by Mark Brazier-Jones. A pair of Goodman Charlton wing chairs helps the office double as a comfortable library.*

**Left** *In the living room, Goodman and Charlton used large-scale pieces as focal points, leaning a Piero Fornasetti panel against the wall like a huge painting. The Siren sofa, exaggerated Wigmore wing chair and the snaky Swerve lamp are among their designs. A mirrored overmantel adds depth to the room; a tall candelabra lends height.*

**Above** *A vintage screen by Piero Fornasetti lends stature to the 150-square-foot master bedroom; Goodman Charlton's tufted Grande Escargot bench adds sculptural seating. The room is subtly expanded by glazed walls, which have more dimension than flat paint.*

BRAD BLAIR

# A Well-Edited Home
### Beverly Hills, California

1,200 square feet/111.48 square meters

Brad Blair is the kind of designer who loves the serenity of a blank wall, the simplicity of bare floorboards. They create a sense of spaciousness in a small home, he says, and are key elements in his own, the top half of a 1920s Mediterranean-style house.

Blair, a designer with Charles Jacobsen, Inc., was looking for the gracious backdrops he considers crucial to small projects. He found them here — thick plaster walls, coved ceilings, elegant moldings. The previous owner had painted each room a different color, a grievance Blair redressed with his own Zen-like palette. It is more intricate than it first appears: a warm gray-beige in the bedrooms, a deeper shade of the same in the living and dining rooms, a grayed celadon on the bedroom ceiling. All are complex colors that vacillate between light and shadow. "Once painted," he says, "the rooms were in harmony. They seem much larger than they really are."

Into this spare setting, he brought furnishings that evoked for him the romantic interiors of colonial India. Most are antiques from China, India and Indonesia, each piece chosen for its stature and slightly primitive quality, and placed at a respectful distance from its neighbor. "A house must be able to breathe," says Blair. "There's something very comforting to the soul in empty space."

**Left & Above** *Blair's front verandah is a dual-purpose space, serving as his sole foyer and alfresco dining room. Indian chick blinds not only offer privacy but imply windows above the railing, suggesting an interior room.*

**Opposite** *A daybed upholstered in Indian douppioni silk can be made up for guests, but also lets the spare bedroom double as a media and reading room. The 18th-century South American clay warriors form a calculated contrast against the gilded mirror frame.*

*Photography by David Glomb*

*In lieu of bureaus in the master bedroom, a refurbished kitchen cupboard from China holds clothing and a television, while socks are stashed in the drawers of diminutive tables by the window. For nightstands, Blair deployed two halves of a Punjabi sandstone arch.*

**Above**  *The living room holds four key furnishings, perfectly balanced: an oversized sofa, dripping fringe; a Punjabi arch fragment used as a table; a Meiji-era Japanese screen and, beneath it, an antique Indian bench. The Japanese paper lantern keeps the lighting soft.*

**Opposite**  *A breakfast room, just off the dining room, is also the designer's home office. The rug runs nearly wall to wall and helps establish the scale of a larger space.*

**Right**  *In the dining room, four 18th-century Indian illustrations are matted in saturated jewel tones, chosen to match upholstery fabric on the chairs. Blinds in the breakfast room beyond are handwoven of bush clover.*

## STAMPS & STAMPS

# Grand Illusions
### Los Angeles, California

1,200 square feet / 111.48 square meters

This 1940s town house had all the sparse moldings and low-slung ceilings of generic, white-box construction. But Odom Stamps, an architect, and his wife, Kate, an interior designer, live in rooms that seem to have been imported from 18th- and 19th-century Europe.

Ignoring the living room's contemporary L shape, Odom and Kate arranged furniture to evoke the proportions of grander surroundings. They anchored one end of the room with a chest-on-chest nearly seven feet tall, visually lifting the ceiling, and counterweighted the other end with a sofa nearly eight feet long. Armchairs are substantial; the dining table, though notched into the ell, is dressed for a more formal space.

Much of the art, however, is delicate. The owners collect 17th- to 19th-century watercolors from England and Italy, which they gather, for stature, into dense, high groupings characteristic of taller rooms. "Overscaled things keep the room from looking miniature," says Kate. "But it's also a balance of large- and small-scaled objects that makes it work. When everything is harmonious, your eye is gently led around the room. The result is a wonderful sense of spaciousness."

**Left** *In a daughter's small bedroom, silk bed-curtains rise to the ceiling. The full-size wing chair consumes an entire corner, but creates a retreat for reading.*

*Photography by Tim Street-Porter*

**Above** *The living room's upholstered bench can hold books or double as seating. The 1920s painting of an interior draws the eye right past the boundary of the wall.*

**Opposite** *A statuesque chest-on-chest, crowned with oversized pieces of Wedgwood, successfully challenges the low ceilings. The stair rail is one of the few architectural details that came with the house.*

**Above**  *The master bedroom holds 14 pieces of furniture, most down-sized so the room does not feel crowded — the round table, for example, is 28 inches wide, not the customary 36.*

**Left**  *A grouping of 19th-century portraits stops at the edge of the open dining area, creating a sense of enclosure. The table wears a Soumak carpet over Colfax & Fowler fabric.*

**Left**  *The master bedroom's French bedstead is a double, not the expected queen. The vintage French chandelier is just jewelry; there's no ceiling outlet. French altar steps are angled into the room to counteract a tight corner.*

**Above & Opposite** *Turning the garden into a semi-enclosed space was a way of extending the house. The "ceiling" consists of passion flowers, which grow on netting that was stretched on the framework of a former awning. The floor is laid with terra cotta tiles.*

# BIERLY-DRAKE

## A Cottage of Character
### Nantucket, Massachusetts

440 square feet/42.3 square meters

**Right** *Bierly and Drake hung an architectural embellishment over the living room's sole painting, an 18th-century Italian landscape, creating a spare but effective focal point. The skirted end-table offers secret storage.*

**Below** *The exterior of the cottage was cleaned, making it look lighter and larger. A patio with table and chairs, seen in the floor plan, adds 400 square feet of outdoor living and dining space.*

*Photography by Sam Gray*

Boston interior designers Lee Bierly and Christopher Drake own one of the smallest dwellings on Nantucket. Because it was built in the 1920s as an artist's studio, it is graced with good proportions and an extravagance of sunlight. But because the artist went home to a grander house, the structure's largest area, the living room, is just 120 square feet.

Bierly and Drake made two alterations, turning a sleeping area into a private bedroom and constructing a sleeping loft for guests. Then they invested in the backdrop. Skinny baseboards were replaced with neat, substantial one-by-fours. Old hardware gave way to black iron hinges and brass knobs, says Bierly, giving a plain cottage its sense of coherence.

The designers unified the walls and floors in their trademark cream-colored paint and then pulled back, putting little into the rooms besides the white Gustavian furniture, light-colored upholstery in cotton and linen, and sisal rugs. "You can easily overwork a small house," says Drake. "But we appreciate space and light. We didn't see the need to accessorize."

**Above** *Built-in cabinets flank the bed. Each has drawers in the base, a wardrobe for hanging clothes, and, under the light, a recessed niche — just big enough for a telephone, a small light and a book.*

**Left** *The designers found the dining room's old metal lighting fixture and painted it white. The hutch, chairs and table (which has a built-in Lazy Susan) are new; the bowfront commode is circa 1840.*

**Right** *The living room was permitted one shot of color, supplied by Portuguese pots in oceanic blue that Bierly and Drake made into lamps. Decorative artist Frederick Browne painted the tole table.*

# ERIC WATSON

## A Lofty Guest House

Seaside, Florida

440 square feet/42.3 square meters

The ironclad esthetic code that governs Seaside, the famous planned community, gave architect Eric Watson just a slip of land — 240 square feet — on which to build a guest house. There, behind the main house, his client wanted to squeeze a self-contained and airy structure.

A visitor's eye would need room to roam, Watson knew, and the only direction available to him was up. He turned the front of the living room into a light well, open to the sky through clerestory windows and soaring 19 feet to a vaulted ceiling. The rest of the room is lowered by a sleeping loft overhead.

Watson had another means of teasing open the space: extraordinary views of the Gulf of Mexico. The house faces east, with four tall windows downstairs marshalled toward the beach, and a balcony that extends the sleeping loft toward the sea. White cotton curtains, almost graphic in their simplicity, hang from galvanized metal rods.

With the main house standing just eight feet away, Watson could place no windows in the long, western wall. He devoted it to cabinetry, stringing kitchen appliances, countertop, and a nearby entertainment unit along its length downstairs. Above, where a windowless bathroom might have felt confined, he walled it in with glass block to draw light from the sunlit stairs.

**Left & Below** *To make this small house look solid, Watson used wide bands of lap-siding on the ground floor, suggesting mass, and narrower bands upstairs. Corner windows make the second floor look lighter, heightening the contrast.*

*Photography by Jack Gardner*

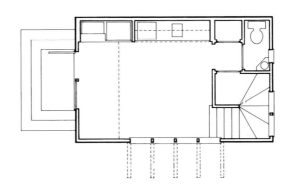

Below   *The living room draws
most of its color from its vistas,
which act as focal points in this
small space. A banded sconce reiterates the horizontal paneling outside, and also contrasts with the
beadboard walls.*

**Above** *A glass front door, uncluttered by mullions, opens into the double-height section of the living room. Pull-up shades offer privacy and partial shade.*

**Right** *A niche in the sleeping loft holds a sink, allowing one guest to wash up while another showers. In this narrow spot, the triple mirror is an unexpected luxury.*

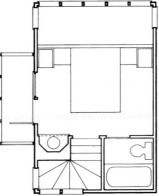

**Above** *Though the loft is only 118 square feet, its perceived volume is pried open by glass doors, the balcony, a bank of windows behind the bed and the high, peaked ceiling. Built in wardrobes and nightstands flank the bed, whose mattress rests on deep storage drawers. Reading lights, bookshelves, outlets and light switches are designed into this wall-to-wall headboard.*

# CAROL OLTEN

## A Cottage Dreamscape
La Jolla, California

1,100 square feet/102.19 square meters

"A fantasy," says interior designer Carol Olten, "isn't limited by square footage." She regards her own rooms as stage sets, which she props with poetic objects — from dozens of vintage gloves to yards of veil-like netting.

The house, a 1916 cottage, had been "severely remuddled," as Olten puts it, with a dark Mediterranean kitchen. A few strokes of renovation increased its sense of space: Olten merged two bathrooms into one, removed a wall between the kitchen and breakfast nook and, in a bedroom-turned-studio, excised the ceiling and inserted two skylights. "The cathedral ceiling adds volume," she says, "and skylights make the space seem larger."

In a progression of colors, her darkest rooms were painted in the deepest shades. "You would expect dark rooms to be painted white," the designer says, "but I think a dark color makes them more inviting." By restricting strong colors to the walls and keeping furniture colors neutral, Olten can pursue her unorthodox mix of styles — from wicker chairs to crystal chandeliers. "Working with a cottage is more appealing to me than a 20,000-square-foot house," she says. "You can make something much more intimate and personal of it."

**Left**  *With artist Jon Patrick Butterworth, Carol Olten painted the Van Gogh-style sunflowers on her picket fence and the fantasy portrait (half Cheshire cat, half Alice) on her chimney.*

*Photography by Russ Gilbert*

**Above**  *Olten designed the slightly Gothic gazebo in her garden as an extra room. It incorporates four 19th-century leaded-glass windows from Scotland that repeat the sunflower motif from her fence.*

**Opposite**  *With its 1920s Italian daybed, the living room doubles as guest quarters. The sofa is a vintage Louis XV reproduction, twig chairs are new, and decoration runs to butterflies painted on the wall and purple faux-marbling on the hearth.*

**Opposite** *To brighten her design studio, Olten painted the rafters glossy white to catch the light. The studio also functions as a formal dining room.*

**Right** *Where some designers might post a bulletin board, Olten created a wall-sized montage. Pale floor-boards were finished with satin polyurethane; like the chandelier, they reflect light, subliminally enlarging the room.*

**Below** *The 1920s breakfast table doubles as Olten's writing desk. The painted frieze of a cat playing with rope is copied from the kitchen's tiled back-splash, designed by ceramic artist Tom Hatton.*

**Above** *To give her white bath-room some distinction, Olten chose furnishings with a high pattern quotient. The mirror was designed by a stained-glass artisan; the Victorian reception chair was designed for an entry hall.*

# RICHAR

## Polished by Light

Michiana Shore, Michigan

1,000 square feet/92.9 square meters

W hen Richar first entered this 1930s split-log cabin, he says, "I thought I was in a treehouse." The walls were lined with wood and bejewelled with knots; the living area, though open, felt intimate. The drawback was darkness. Sunshine barely penetrated the place, and the wood had grown dull — but this was a gloom that Richar knew he could dispel.

His primary instrument was light. Into a ceiling that reaches 24 feet at its peak, Richar inserted four skylights, two above the living room and two over a second-story sleeping loft. His painter cleaned the paneling, which was sullied by years of smoke from the hearth, and waxed it, so it glowed under daylight and firelight. Where curtains were needed, they were made of creamy wool that let natural light slip through. Finally, Richar painted all of the ceilings pale blue, as if the sky were mirrored there.

His Arts and Crafts furnishings have a handsome, brooding quality that required some relief. This came in the form of reproduction lighting, which repeats the severe designs but makes them luminous; and silver-white birch furniture, which Richar designed. The cabin's interior now feels like a piece of amber — not bright, but burnished to a fine glow.

**Above** *Richar designed strapping furnishings — including tilt-and-swivel chairs covered in horsehair — to balance the living room's two-story fieldstone hearth. A Berber cape hangs above the window, bringing color to the upper reaches of the room.*

**Left** *Richar enclosed a screened-in porch to add more living space in winter. Confronted with brown-painted wood in this room, he painted it again — this time with faux bois grain and knots.*

*Photography by James Yochum*

*The living room appears to have been furnished straight from the woods: antlers on the posts, a buffalo head over the hearth, a wintry tree captured in the Chuck Walker oil painting. The link to nature helps dissolve the cabin's tight boundaries.*

**Above** *Richar converted a guest closet to a small bath, glazing its walls to resemble Teco pottery from the same era as the house. He made the mirror's frame of birch and cherry branches and affixed it to an ordinary medicine cabinet.*

**Left** *In the sleeping loft, birch beds designed by Richar have the overscaled proportions and the light coloration that the upper level demanded. Every piece of furniture or art is illuminated from the rafters by a track light.*

**Above** *Lacking a dining room, the table was given its own enclave by the front door. The setting is brightened not only by glass doors, but by the table's white-birch pedestal and the cowhide rug beneath.*

**Opposite** *The guest-room bed, made in Mexico of metal with a leather headboard, is an antidote to a tight space: The sculpted trees at each corner give the ceiling a lift and make the room unexpectedly airy.*

# ACE ARCHITECTS

## The Diminutive Cathedral

Oakland Hills, California

1,200 square feet/111.48 square meters

It is impossible to feel cramped by a small house when your living room vaults to a height of 26 feet, or when your stair-landing is a balcony that soars over this celestial space. That was precisely the intention: Make one room magnanimous, explain David Weingarten and Lucia Howard, partners in Ace Architects, and the rest of the house will not suffer from tight proportions.

The living room is anchored by a massive hearth, and sparsely furnished. Its strongest decoration comes from architectural details, such as the arched newel posts and pendant lights that recapitulate the vaulted shape. The room funnels into smaller spaces, setting up evocative and deliberate contrasts: On one side of the balcony, four steps turn a corner and form the stairwell; on the other side, four matching steps ascend to a niche barely big enough for its chair and writing desk. The three bedrooms range from only 100 to 144 square feet.

"What really makes a big room feel spacious is to come to it through a small room," says Weingarten. "And nothing makes a small room feel so intimate as to reach it through a vast one."

He drew the living room's palette from tiles in San Simeon, the fabled William Randolph Hearst estate. "Having the luxury of seven colors in one room complements the luxury of having this very tall space," Weingarten says. "The colors make the house complex — and complexity is a true luxury in a small home."

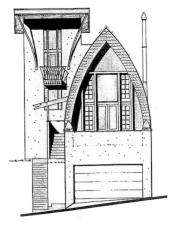

**Above**  *The towering Gothic arch, an overriding motif in the architecture of this new house, reappears in curved supports under the eaves and, on a smaller scale, by the ironwork on a small balcony railing.*

**Opposite**  *The arched structure houses the living room, where an interior balcony serves as a stair-landing. The owner's daughter must cross it to reach her room at the top of an adjoining tower.*

*Photography by Alan Weintraub*

Left *The kitchen opens onto a dining room, which feeds onto a private terrace. Curved posts are a gentle reminder of the living room's powerful arch. Animated plywood chairs were designed by the architects.*

Below *At the foot of the hearth, a patchwork of tiles includes every color used throughout the house. Above the mantel are copper-faced asphalt shingles — the same type used on the vaulted roof, where they were chemically weathered to a green patina.*

Opposite *A tall hearth, clad in coppery tiles, and the broad mantel underscore the living room's formidable dimensions.*

# GUY STANSFELD

## Reclaiming the Attic
London, England

790 square feet/73.39 square meters

Guy Stansfeld's client had a theatrical sense of style — and a decidedly plain mews house in which to exercise it. Built in the 1960s, it consisted of a ground-floor garage, second-story living quarters, and an attic hospitable only to suitcases.

Money was too tight for an addition, but the owner, rock musician Tony James, had budgeted for one dramatic, architectural gesture. Stansfeld used it to open the interior horizons of the little house, carving out a loftlike living room and replacing the attic with a mezzanine.

With its old ceiling gone, the front of the living room now soars almost to the roof. Construction materials, from steel girders to a concrete supporting wall, were left exposed — partly for their industrial good looks, partly to lower costs. Brick walls were shorn of their plaster and sealed, and a new floor was laid of inexpensive plywood that Stansfeld cut into broad rectangles, set on the diagonal and varnished. The hard-edged effect of plywood and concrete is softened by fantastical lighting fixtures, designed by James to shed a melting yellow light.

Once the space was teased open, the architect built a storage wall consisting almost entirely of doors. A few open onto other rooms; the rest conceal cupboards. Painted purple, the wall reads as a solid plane. By concealing most of the owner's belongings, it also preserves the airy sensibility of his home.

*Left* *A redesign of the white mews house included a steely new facade, with nautical hardware, a porthole for the door, and an industrial garage door. These diverse elements are united by the band that runs above them like a valance.*

*Photography by José King*

*Above* *On the mezzanine, sky-lights illuminate a knee-wall of storage cabinetry. The vertical panel marshals switches, outlets and television controls into a futuristic-looking column.*

*Opposite* *The owner designed the flame-colored parchment sconces and chose all of the loft's colors, including a lipstick red paint that exalts the angular forms of girders and stairs.*

**Left** *Under the mezzanine, icono-graphic thrones designed by the owner hold court around a dining table. Purple doors and the sur-rounding wall were painted alike, unifying the backdrop.*

**Below** *The narrow rooftop garden was made possible when half of the peaked roof was lifted, creating headroom for the mezzanine below. Strong shots of color in the painted furniture establish a link with the interior.*

# CARL D'AQUINO

## Habitat for an Artist
### New York City

1,200 square feet/111.48 square meters

When this narrow town house was built in 1858, it had arched mantels, broad doorways, and a curving stair that ran through its core like a spine. Its dignity stayed intact for a century, too, before someone carved it into a boardinghouse.

Designer Carl D'Aquino laid bare the original refinement with only minor surgery, realigning doorways and hauling out wallboard partitions. His clients — Nicholas Howey, an artist, and Gerard Wittershoven, a dealer of art deco furnishings — wanted a home for their collections as well as for themselves; and in deference to the artworks, D'Aquino might logically have given them a gallery, neutralized with a five-story coat of white paint. Instead he painted each room its own rich color, so that a visitor perceives this underscaled house as affording many moods and surroundings. "I wanted you to experience each room," D'Aquino explains, "as if you were walking into a painting."

On the ground floor, visitors are met in a red vestibule and ushered through a pumpkin foyer and living room. One flight up is the cobalt dining room, whose stormy walls Howey created with pigment-rich theatrical paint. The guest suite is emerald, with a yellow ceiling; the master bedroom, at the top, is paper-bag tan, the most meditative hue in the house. "The progression of colors," says D'Aquino, "brings a certain order to the house."

**Opposite** *The foyer gets its commanding presence from period furnishings and artworks: Pierre Cazaubon statue, Paul Klee rug, and century-old French jacquard curtains.*

**Below** *D'Aquino made the central staircase into a five-story kaleidoscopic sculpture, covering its steps with remnants of movie-theatre carpeting. "It makes the stairwell into a room," the designer says.*

*Photography by Thibault Jeanson*

**Right** *The kitchen's 1928 breakfast table was salvaged from a Brooklyn cocktail lounge. A tiered skyscraper bookcase by Paul Theodore Frankl makes a freestanding pantry.*

**Left & Above**  *Anchoring the living room is Donna Moylan's painting, "The House of Dreams"; the round portrait is Robert Loughlin's "Dock Worker." The Bruno Paul carpet and angular Francis Jourdain armchair are early-20th-century classics; the Thebes stool from 1880 is upholstered in parchment.*

**Above**  *The library is one of two rooms in the green suite, where guests sleep. A Robert Rauschenberg silkscreen hangs over the fireplace; the rug was designed by Alexander Calder.*

**Above & Right** *The dining room, small as a ship's cabin, is made boundless by its stormy cobalt walls. The 1920s chairs are by Louis Majorelle, the vase is by Just Anderson. Stephen Downes, a New York artist, sculpted the curtain tieback.*

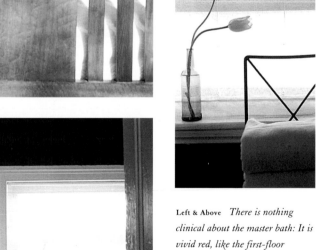

Left  *The fifth floor master bedroom stretched to 16 feet after several small rooms were merged. The furnishings, possibly Wiener Werkstatte, have nickel detailing on wood; the painting is by Nicholas Howey.*

Below left  *Because the bedroom was originally a garret, its windows, hung with a period linen print, are at floor level. All of the paintings are by Nicholas Howey.*

Left & Above  *There is nothing clinical about the master bath: It is vivid red, like the first-floor vestibule, so the house starts and ends in the same color. Its luxury lies in being furnished as a real room, with muslin shades, Printz shelf, Art Deco lighting and a rug.*

# DONALD MAXCY DESIGN

## By Serenity Enlarged
Monterey, California

1,100 square feet/102.19 square meters

The angular architecture was pure 1950s, but this one-story home, recently purchased by two interior designers, was redeemed by graces from an earlier era. Its ceilings were uncharacteristically lofty, nearly 10 feet high, and a phalanx of tall windows gave every room a glass wall onto the garden.

Donald and Marsha Maxcy, partners in a design firm as well as in marriage, gained some living space by consolidating a sprawling, open kitchen into a manageable 130 square feet. But their key strategy was to create a monochromatic interior and let the garden views visually extend it. With linen-white paint, they relieved the darkness of brick and redwood-paneled walls. Fabrics and furnishings are overscaled, tricking the eye into perceiving a larger room, and most are in shades of cream or bone so that they blend in with the neutral surroundings. "There's no high contrast of color," says Donald Maxcy. "It would shrink the rooms."

Against this restful backdrop, excitement is engendered by textural contrasts: bronze near bamboo, lacquer near wood, rice paper near stone. Natural, high-touch materials have replaced ornament in this house, and it is no accident that the result is distinctly Japanese in style. "Oriental design creates a sense of order," says Maxcy, "and expands your perception of space."

**Above**  *Allusions to nature give the dining room its link to the garden and obscure its awkward shape. Bronze sconces were cast in molds made from branches; a woven bamboo screen hides stereo equipment.*

*Photography by Marco P. Zecchin, Image Center*

**Opposite**  *To reach the front door, visitors cross a footbridge over a dried streambed carpeted with stones. The master bedroom is to the left, living room to the right.*

**Overleaf**  *The guest room, also a media room, contains a bed as low as a Japanese altar. For textural contrasts, Maxcy installed the papery Isamu Noguchi lamp and two Native American grinding stones.*

# DOREE FRIEDMAN

## Liberating Tight Space
Berkeley, California

1,149 square feet/106.74 square meters

Ninety years ago, this house conveyed its modest grace through leaded windows, high baseboards and polished blond floors. But to Doree Friedman, a designer and builder, its six rooms also had a boxy esthetic that was smothering some of the charm.

Rather than reconfigure the one-story house, which proceeded logically from the old front door to the new redwood deck, Friedman architecturally aired it out. She replaced interior doorways with broader openings, cut tall and wide so the public rooms practically fused. One of these portals was given new moldings to match the room around it; others, devoid of doors, were left surgically bare around the edges. Deep, interior windows, freshly cut between the living and dining rooms, lengthen the views within the house and add to the perception of space.

Friedman planned the lighting so that small areas could be isolated and engagingly lit. She painted or plastered some of the walls in muted yellows and ochers, and replaced plain doors with antique ones salvaged in Santa Fe. Their wood, rubbed with use, brings some patina to this updated home. "It's elegant, but also comfortable," says Friedman, "because the rooms feel open and intimate at the same time."

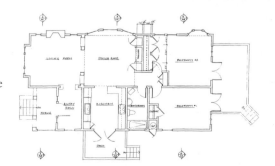

**Above** *An antique New England bench sets off the entry hall's architectural detailing, original to the 1906 house. The lighting fixture was designed by the owner with Ocean View Lighting.*

*Photography by Beatriz Coll*

**Opposite** *Spanish Colonial doors, with a display shelf for a lintel, make a rugged facade for a linen closet. Friedman lowered the hallway ceiling, creating a sheltered space that pours into the taller dining room.*

Above *Glass doors, installed by a previous owner, give the master bedroom and adjoining library their sweeping connection to the outdoors. Friedman designed the clean-cut nightstands to melt into the background, focusing attention on the art.*

**Below** *New, built-in storage keeps the dining room spare. The diminutive Mexican door with the hinged panel is from an old church confessional; one of a pair, it now conceals stereo equipment.*

**Above** *Friedman stripped a once-incommodious bath of its floor-to-ceiling gray tiles, then opened the room up with lighter colors: a pale floor of tumbled marble, ocher tilework around the shower. An oversized mirror doubles the interior views.*

# BRUCE BIERMAN

## Master of Its Views
### Fire Island, New York

750 square feet/72.1 square meters

To a visitor, this contemporary beach cottage is hardly constricted by its walls — not when every room unfurls onto a deck, and addresses the ocean through glass doors. But on paper, the two-bedroom house is smaller than some studio apartments.

What its measurements don't reveal is that Bruce Bierman, the designer and owner, virtually lives on the four decks that double his square footage. And they don't convey the way every seat in the house is angled to face the sea: "Wherever you sit," says Bierman, "you feel expanded by the ocean. No piece of furniture turns its back on the view."

On the decks, chaise lounges and butterfly chairs are dressed in white. And the interiors themselves, spare as driftwood, are stripped of inessential belongings. Each bedroom contains little more than a white bed and a glass wall, and in the living room no side-tables are tucked between the chairs. "I designed the house much as I would a yacht," says Bierman. "When space is at a premium, everything should have a purpose and a place."

**Opposite** *The beds, like everything else in the house and on the deck, wear white, as Bierman felt that contrast would visually shrink the space. Rafters are painted white as well, to keep the ceiling visually aloft.*

**Left & Below** *The coffee table, which Bierman made of salvaged wood, stands only 12 inches high to emphasize a ceiling that rises to 13 feet — and to serve as a footrest, too. Sofa cushions are grandly overscaled to make the room feel generous.*

*Photography Courtesy of Bruce Bierman*

**Far Left** *To avoid the touch-me-not effect of perfectly folded towels, Bierman hangs them from metal hooks on a strip of wood. Soaps are gathered in a primitive wooden trough for textural contrast with the contemporary sink.*

**Left** *At bedside, Artemide's Berenice halogen lamp can be aimed at the ceiling for ambient light, or angled toward the pages of a book; its blue glass shade reiterates the ocean outside.*

**Above** *At nine feet square, the two identical bedrooms are not much bigger than Victorian trunk rooms. Their horizons, however, are extended by a glass door on one wall, mirrored panels on another.*

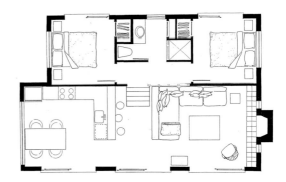

**Above & Right** *The four decks that encircle the house are extensions of its rooms, and furnished accordingly. Just off the living room and kitchen, butterfly chairs congregate around a 12-inch-high coffee table — just as low-slung as the one inside. This one, however, is not square, but angles out toward the water.*

## MACNELLY • COHEN

# A Nautical Economy of Space
Vineyard Haven, Massachusetts

1,170 square feet/108.7 square meters

**Opposite** *Bruce MacNelly, the architect's husband and partner, designed the curving cupboards and ceiling in a fantasy chamber adjoining the guest room. Over this wave-like armature, Richard Iammarino painted the seascape. The chair is from MacKenzie Childs.*

The buyer had lived on boats. The architect, Linda Joy Cohen, worked over a boatyard. And the house presented the kind of tight, tricky spaces that can confound a yacht designer — constricted doorways, seven-foot ceilings, stairs nearly as steep as a ship's ladder.

Indeed, Cohen knew that this weekend refuge could be expanded only by light, views, and interior space. She allowed one room to sprawl by merging the kitchen and dining room into a 330-square-foot gathering spot, which she pried open even further by tearing out its ceiling, and installing French doors, skylights, and an arched bay window. All other rooms kept their low ceilings. "In 19th-century Beaux Arts architecture, it was very desirable to contrast tall, open spaces with intimate ones," says Cohen. "In its modest way, this house tries to achieve that."

Downstairs, she stole a square sitting room to make a divertimento, a little diversion. A painted seascape meanders across every surface of the room. "In a small house," says Cohen, "it's important to be able to sit by yourself and just take a deep breath."

**Left** *The 1950s cottage suggests a cozy, 18th-century Cape Cod house.*

**Above** *In the master bedroom, an interior window looks over the kitchen rafters. A quirk that survived the renovation, it was formerly a hatch door to the attic.*

**Left** *Cohen gutted a small room that had been lined with bunk beds to create this private sitting area.*

*Photography by
Robert Schellhammer (above & opposite),
David Lund (left & far left)*

# An Orderly Cottage
Ogunquit, Maine

401 square feet/37.25 square meters

Deep in the woods, yet close to the ocean, Boston designer Gregory Cann found a vintage, three-room cabin of unfinished pine. (The third room, he explains, is the porch.) "I liked its compactness," says Cann, "and it had good bones. Even the wood interior had rustic charm — for about two nights."

He wrapped every surface in Benjamin Moore's Antique White, a paint shade with pink undertones to counter the gray winter days. The bed wears white; a collection of 19th-century prints have white grounds and white mats; even the broad floorboards are white, as are bits of gingerbread that trim the rooms. "Your eye doesn't have much to track, so you get the impression of more space," says Cann. "I'm very aware of the difference between claustrophobic and cozy."

Prints, plates and architectural embellishments hang on the walls in compositions that reveal an inner discipline. "I arrange things so that they snap into a grid," says Cann. "Blue and white plates are framed by the gable. Pictures over the window align with a piece of molding." As for knowing when to stop, he adheres to Diana Vreeland's famous counsel: When you are all dressed up, pause at the door on your way out — and take one thing off.

**Above** *Cann designed a new entry with French doors and a portico. The doors bring sunlight into a house canopied by trees, and make the subtle conversion from cabin to cottage.*

**Left** *The 200-square-foot porch is furnished with a coffee table and other indoor comforts; lunch is served on oval plates that fit the Adirondack chairs' broad arms.*

**Opposite** *The main room is host to cooking, dining, relaxing, and guests. An antique egg crate makes a diminutive coffee table that holds linens for the sofabed; low shutters offer privacy while admitting light.*

*Photography by Eric Roth*

Left  *Suspended from vines, a patchwork-quilt headboard is backed by insulation, cotton batting and foam, all upholstered to the wall. A bureau doubles as a nightstand.*

Below left & Right  *A crocheted cloth drapes the table; chairs are intentionally mismatched, though wedded by their floral cushions and spindled backs.*

Opposite  *Working in the Arts and Crafts style, Cann nailed a design of bittersweet vines to his kitchen cabinetry. By painting them white, he could infuse the cottage with pattern and rhythm, yet never flirt with clutter.*

"I stretch the size of a small apartment by building everything in — bookshelves, media cabinet, drawers under the bed." ~ *David Rockwell*

*apartments*

# TRANSIT DESIGN

## Bringing a Terrace Indoors
### Rome, Italy

700 square feet/65.03 square meters

Within the shell of a venerable building stands the skeleton of a modern, one-bedroom apartment. Its walls are newly minted, with built-in shelves. Its doorways are tall and untrimmed, as if cut by surgeons. Nearly 14 feet overhead, however, floats a wooden ceiling that may date back to 1800.

A key purpose of the update was to enhance the connection with two terraces. The architects literally did it with mirrors — four in the living room alone, exactly as tall as the interior doorways, and sometimes covering the doors. Artfully positioned, says Danilo Parisio, a Transit partner, "The mirrors re-propose the terrace views, which refutes the limited interior space."

The new walls are not seamlessly melded to the old; instead, they stand about four inches in front, and stop short of the ceiling. This leaves the uppermost band of the original walls quite visible. The Transit partners painted the band black, highlighting a mysterious gap between old and new construction, and underscoring the split between the centuries. One result is that a visitor perceives the structure as a new liner in an aged container and becomes conscious of the apartment as a whole, not as a collection of rooms.

The white backdrop emphasizes the modernity, and defers to the planted terraces. "This way," explains Parisio, "the windows are like paintings. They have no competition."

**Above** *The living room, entirely rebuilt, contrasts a square and stark fireplace with the traditional round window of attic apartments in Rome. Black accents, like Transit's sofa table, keep the room crisp.*

**Opposite** *A small dining area occupies a corner of the living room. Architectural elements, such as the radiator grille and window frame, are modernized; furnishings include antiques, like the Biedermeier chairs.*

*Photography by Janos Grapow*

1 LIVING-DINING    3 TERRACE    5 CLOSET    7 BATHROOM
2 KITCHEN          4 BEDROOM    6 BOUDOIR

**Right**  *To create a hospitable pause where no foyer exists, a lacquered console table attends the mirrored front door. A second mirrored door leads to the bedroom.*

**Left**  *The bath is enlarged by mirrors and set apart by curtains, making its boundaries fluid.*

**Below**  *The bedroom has a private terrace. What appears to be a high, round window into another part of the interior is in fact, just a circle of mirror.*

*Photography by*
*Pietro Mari (right),*
*Janos Grapow (left & below)*

Left *Windowshades can be low-ered on the terrace, creating a semi-interior space. The fountain is a mix of the modern and the antique, much like the rooms inside.*

*Photography by Pietro Mari*

Left *For privacy, the architects redesigned the main terrace as a room, with high terra-cotta walls, an iron framework, and a ceiling of moveable fabric panels.*

Above *A bathroom window filters sunlight through sandblasted glass. The circle in the middle is mirrored inside.*

## MARY DOUGLAS DRYSDALE

## Reaching for the View

Washington, D.C.

850 square feet/78.97 square meters

Coaxing four rooms into 850 square feet probably took all the developer's art. Mary Drysdale's job was to undo it — the divisive floor plan, the rooms with no view, the hemmed-in kitchen. "As you walked in," She says, "you saw drywall, not terrace."

She altered the layout like a surgeon, removing obstructions to circulation and view. The living room and den merged. A kitchen wall fell, replaced by an island. And a second bedroom doorway was carved, hinting that two chambers, not one, lay beyond the living room. When the dust settled, the kitchen, bedroom and foyer had their first views of the terrace.

The decoration, like the businessman who lives here part-time, is tailored and restrained. Drysdale paneled one living-room wall in oak, bleached and glazed until it was luminous, and overlaid it with a wooden grid. The other walls are Sheetrock, but the grid wraps around them all the same. "With my budget, I couldn't panel the whole room," says Drysdale, "but I could express the grid differently."

So seamless is the pale backdrop, with its bleached floors and ivory fabrics, that the eight-foot ceilings seem to drift to another altitude. The result is a room so composed that it required a note of rebellion — in this case, a dining table with a sinuous, metal web of a base. "The grid," says Drysdale, "is formal and controlled. The table is the absolute contradiction."

**Above** *Drysdale designed the foyer's lacquered demilune table, launching a pattern of black accents throughout the apartment.*

**Opposite** *A second, newly opened doorway between living room and bedroom gives the bed — placed discreetly out of sight — its terrace view. Hardware for the living-room sheers is hidden in a drapery pocket.*

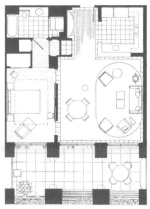

**Above** *New kitchen cabinets were stained to match the living room's oak wall, uniting the two rooms. A tray ceiling, created during renovation, adds dimension and height.*

**Overleaf** *The bedroom wallcovering is a paper-backed wood veneer — geometric, but less severe than the living room's gridded walls. A round mirror adds breadth to a room just $9^1/_2$ feet wide.*

## CARL D'AQUINO

## Governed by Proportion
### New York City

450 square feet/41.81 square meters

At the top of a pre–Civil War building, Carl D'Aquino welcomes the embrace of four small rooms. "I like the scale," he says. "It makes me feel protected. The proportions are perfect, and that makes it restful."

The foyer, in the center of the apartment, is a true square. Flanked by two other rooms, it creates an enfilade through broad doorways that visually binds the terrace, at one end, to the bedroom, at the other. No renovation was needed, save the removal of some baseboards so that a 10-foot Portuguese armoire could slide into its niche in the foyer. "The sensibility of how you are choreographed through a space is primary to me," says D'Aquino, who realigns doorways in his clients' homes the way some people rearrange furniture. "I use objects and vistas to draw your eye up and through the rooms, the way artists used to hang paintings above other paintings."

The all-white backdrop is rare for him, but it underscores the modern art and slightly eccentric furnishings. It also lets a visitor's eye explore the changes in altitude, from the foyer's vaulted skylight to the slope of the living room ceiling. The sofa is tucked under a narrow but sheltering eave; nearby sits a child's chair, at times called into use as a side table. "I buy pieces for their sculptural lines," says D'Aquino. "But in a small home, everything has to have a purpose."

**Above** *D'Aquino rebuilt the foyer's armoire with double hanging and shelves; the sisal rug is his design. Rectangular sculpture by James Magee; round sculpture by Paul Laird; screen by Caroline Casey.*

**Right** *In the living room, two Portuguese art deco craftsman chairs make an interesting marriage, rather than a matched pair — as do their attendant Thebes and Irish stools.*

*Photography by Andrew Bordwin*

**Opposite** *A 19th-century settee, made in Egypt in the French style, is a rich counterpoint to the bedroom's spare aesthetic. Six-part sculpture of metal, wood and shattered glass by James Magee.*

**Right** *A mirror in the foyer reflects an 18th-century chair occupied by a Kim Uchiyama painting. Above it hangs a painting by Dan Josephs.*

**Above** *D'Aquino describes his American Empire bed as "an event"; for contrast, the room around it is necessarily clean-lined. A lithe German table with a hammered copper top serves as a nightstand.*

**Left** *Circular forms connect the living room's Portuguese art deco chair, 1950s Miami coffee table, and convocation of chairs in the Louise Lawler photograph. Painting by David Yih.*

# GORALNICK ★ BUCHANAN & W. JUDE LEBLANC

## The Glass Addition
### New York City

900 square feet/83.61 square meters

It was the proverbial bowling alley — 65 feet long, just 12 feet wide, and unfurnishable, recall architects Barry Goralnick and Jude LeBlanc. Searching desperately for elbow room, they found it outside: a 3-foot-deep ledge spanning the length of the loft that could, in a feat of engineering, be brought indoors.

They captured it with a steel and glass greenhouse addition, built of prefabricated sections. It makes a dramatic container for the skyline views. "There's such visual splendor in that panorama," says Michael Buchanan, an interior designer and Goralnick's partner, "that we restrained ourselves inside. City, sky and nighttime lights are the only colors the apartment needs."

The enclosure widened the loft to 15 feet, allowing it to be segmented gracefully into rooms — or, in the renovation language that evolved, pavilions. The central living room is flanked by the bedroom pavilion at one end, dining pavilion at the other. The greenhouse runs along it all, a glass-walled corridor. "Now that you move from space to space," says Goralnick, "the apartment loses all sense of being a sliver."

A surprising amount of floorspace was filched for closets, allowing the owner to edit down his furnishings. Little remains in sight besides a few antiques and a pair of chaises, and they are no competition for the cityscape on the other side of the glass.

**Above** *The far ends of the greenhouse were constructed with the loft's original 1920s windows, salvaged during renovation and rebuilt; Juliet balconies were added.*

**Right** *A new foyer, barely large enough for two, formalizes the entryway and creates a counterpoint to the sprawling loft beyond. Interior windows scoop sunlight from the bedroom.*

*Photography by Gary Rogers*

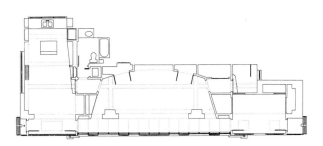

**Above** *Floorboards were laid on the diagonal, adding a third, intriguing dimension to the loft's narrow configuration. Walls were glazed an atmospheric white.*

**Left** *The greenhouse appears to have been clipped onto the loft like a balcony. In contrast to its long and narrow walkway, the rest of the space feels larger.*

**Left**  *The kitchen is also the loft's sole dining room, and with a television installed, it makes an informal gathering spot. The farm table and rattan chairs had to be overscaled, lest they be dwarfed by the massive windows.*

**Below**  *A sofa in the dining area makes the kitchen versatile: It offers seating during parties, or a solitary place to read. A niche was designed around the owner's antique armoire, which holds linens; a discreet panel above it offers extra storage.*

**Right** *The owner, who works in media, wanted a television in every room; the designers avoided cabinetry by mounting sleek, black units on the walls. A high ratio of glass and mirror to solid wall keeps the room from feeling as small as it is — just 80 square feet.*

**Below** *Opposite the living room's greenhouse window, Goralnick and Buchanan designed a curved wall — partly for architectural interest, but also because the curve makes room for a closet at each end.*

**Above** *The bedroom is packed with hidden storage. One of the tall, mirrored panels that flank the bed is a closet door. Most of the panels near the ceiling also open onto storage, but three are panes of one-way mirror that usher light into the foyer.*

# GALAL MAHMOUD
## Rooms With a View
Paris, France

600 square feet/55.74 square meters

**Left** *The bedroom's aqua carpet makes an airy backdrop. Mirrored panels reiterate those in the living room and reflect light, enlarging the space.*

**Below** *The closet-sized bar, a secondary gathering spot, faces the terrace on one side and reflects it with mirrors on the other.*

*Photography by Jean Etienne Fortunier*

In this white glove building, decades ago, maids lived in cubicles on the highest floor. Now prized by renovators, those turn-of-the-century quarters are often strung into apartments like this — a one-bedroom with four small but flowing rooms, and an Eiffel Tower view to make up for its size.

Ripping out nonstructural walls, architect Galal Mahmoud sculpted a long apartment, rather like a railroad flat, that ends in a generous terrace. As a result, the living room is blessed with light and vistas, but Mahmoud still had to wrestle with its narrow dimensions. For the illusion of depth, he arranged panels of mirror on one wall — copying the evocative proportions of the windows of an artist's atelier. The mirrors reflect the Eiffel Tower, and repeat its glittering lights at night. Brooding colors were banished; turquoise carpeting rolls unexpectedly past the living room and onto the terrace (where a weatherproof version was used).

Mahmoud was confronted by one stubborn niche off the living room: an antiquated bath with a vaulted ceiling. That vault was the apartment's one exotic chord, and he played it up — painting it like a twilit sky, and framing it with an arched doorway. The nook itself, a bonus space, he turned into a sheltered bar for two.

**Above** *Only three colors appear in the living room, but fabrics are mismatched with spirit. Cabana colors disguise the economy of a store-bought sofa and copies of Louis XVI-style chairs.*

**Right** *A Mexican-inspired console table, designed by Mahmoud and his New York partner Jean-Pierre Heim, anchors the living room like a hearth. Sconces keep corners from melting into shadow.*

# TRANSIT DESIGN

## Reshaping History

Ostuni, Italy

915 square feet/85 square meters

**Opposite** *A mirrored screen reflects the living room and shapes a new passageway to the kitchen, whose arched opening is visible above it. The glass table establishes both a foyer and dining area.*

**Left** *A chimney towers over the rooftop terrace. Surrounding houses are repainted each year to keep the historic area pristine.*

**Below** *The living room's new limestone floor matches an old, curving stairway — doubled by its own reflection — that sweeps up to a private terrace.*

*Photography by Janos Grapow*

How do you update a centuries-old structure without disfiguring history? "You cannot change it," says Danilo Parisio, one of four Transit partners who worked around the architecture — part Greek, part Arab, part Spanish — of this two-bedroom home. "But you can present it differently."

The apartment, in a 17th-century old-town district, had not been revamped for 90 years. Its kitchen consisted of a cooking hearth; its bath was a water closet. The architects built both — but their real renovation was achieved with modernist screens and doors set with mirror and blue glass. These reflective planes trap sunlight and slice across corners at intriguing angles; some suggest thresholds into unexplored rooms.

With the insertion of this glass-and-metal framework, the living room feels larger, and free of period constraints. The screens counter the Baroque vaults and arches with "a modern and synthetic language," Parisio says, yet the antiquity of the place remains assertive.

Underfoot, an aged mosaic floor had partly crumbled away. Where restoration proved impossible, the architects laid down limestone. A seam now courses between the two, along which design ideas separated by hundreds of years are both contrasted and fused.

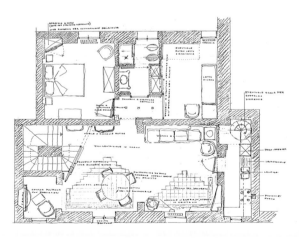

**Above**  *Glass furnishings, including the living room's transparent bookshelves, take up no visual space; a visitor's attention goes straight to the vaulted ceilings and mirrored doors.*

**Left**  *A door of blue glass, its metal framework a distillation of Mackintosh style, leads to the bedroom and bath. Eighteenth-century chairs are displayed like sculpture when not used for dining.*

**Above** *With a hearth blazing near-by and a rug-sized tract of mosaic underfoot, the dining area can feel almost like a separate room.*

**Above** *A mirrored door, set at an angle to better reflect the master bedroom, conceals a recessed closet. Except for the stark absence of embroidery, linen draperies are typical of the region.*

**Opposite** *The bedroom's Italian art deco armoire, suitably massive for the space, brings its own mirrors to the mix. Beyond: the blue glass door to the living room.*

# GORALNICK ★ BUCHANAN

## Rooms Without Corners
New York City

1,100 square feet/102.19 square meters

**Below** *The foyer, a lone rectangle in an apartment of rounded rooms, is anchored by a Victorian hat rack and chair. As the walls are not curved, they made this space a natural gallery.*

Apartments in the fabled Ansonia building have a great design oddity: oval rooms. "Even the ceiling coves are curved," says Barry Goralnick, who recently lived and worked in this two-bedroom rental. But oval rooms, though lyrical, run smaller (no corners). They also resist furniture.

Goralnick, an architect, and Michael Buchanan, a designer, layered jewel-toned fabrics against the living room's paper-bag-colored walls, and mixed antiques with rugs and tables of their own designs. The result is one part modern and two parts baroque, more disciplined than one may realize.

For Buchanan, the wallpaper border was critical. "It brings the 12-foot ceiling into reach," he says, "giving you a human relationship to the room." In addition, the border subtly divides the room into zones: "The furniture height declares the first zone," Buchanan says. "Then your eye jumps to the artwork, then to the chandelier, then to the crown molding. This is how a room begins to make sense."

The master bedroom suggested a hat box to Goralnick. He sponged its sides in a diamond pattern, as if papering it; the lid, or ceiling, is lavender. Deep colors play against this muted backdrop — a lesson, says Buchanan, drawn from 18th-century European painting.

**Above**  *A veil of bronze-colored organza defines the living room window without obscuring it. Other touches of gold — including the legs of the Louix XV-style glass coffee table — convey opulence and reflect light.*

**Right**  *In a room with no real front or sides, the massive Empire sofa provides a point of orientation.*

**Far right**  *A balanced composition on the walls adds to the sofa's prominence, and draws the eye up. The 19th-century portrait is of an actor dressed as Hamlet.*

*Photography by Gary Rogers*

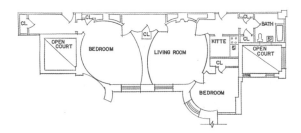

**Right** *The master bedroom's only window was drawn into an intimate niche with the 1930s desk. Goralnick gold-leafed the reproduction Directoire-style chair.*

**Below left & Below** *Two diamond patterns — on the harlequin walls and, more loosely, on the Goralnick ★ Buchanan rug with its border of chairs — help expand this encapsulated space.*

**Opposite** *The bed, a copy of one owned by Napolean, is placed sideways, an arrangement that opens up floorspace and gives the bedroom some of the dignity of a study. The mirror is also a copy; the original was used on a Cecil B. DeMille movie set.*

**Opposite** *The flat side of a demi-lune hallway is lined with books, many of them serving an office in the second bedroom.*

**Below** *The bath came with art deco-era tiles in a vivid green. Goralnick overshadowed them, painting walls and ceiling a darker green, and hanging photographs to draw the eye up.*

**Above** *An American Empire bureau is flanked by a pair of Orion sconces designed by the firm.*

**Right** *The living room required a dining table that wouldn't look domestic, particularly as clients were likely to sit there. Two arm-chairs (rather than a quartet of dining chairs) create the formal setting; the Endymion table, designed by Goralnick ★ Buchanan, is of mahogany, satinwood and ebony.*

## AGNES BOURNE & RICHARD STACY

# The Height Report

San Francisco, California

900 square feet/83.6 square meters

Newly built, this two-bedroom condominium was modeled after old industrial lofts in every way but one: It is a sliver, just 14 feet wide. Yet architect and designer had to delineate six zones while keeping the place from looking like a shoebox.

The layout brought complexity and grace to a difficult space. Architect Richard Stacy planted the kitchen dead-center, which divided the main floor into two discrete rooms. Above the kitchen he set a small, two-bedroom mezzanine, from which the owners can see out the windows at each end of the loft.

Designer Marc Melvin, then at Agnes Bourne, Inc., liked the way the kitchen made an intimate passage between the double-height living and media rooms downstairs. That image became central to his lighting plan, for when the kitchen's shoji-screen doors are closed at night and its light left on, the papery doors glow like lanterns.

Under the mezzanine, bare-board ceilings are only eight feet high. But the living room soars to 22 feet: "The height distracts from the narrowness," Melvin says. "You're always glancing through tall windows, and seeing sky."

**Above & Opposite** *The media room's Chevy sofa, designed by Agnes Bourne, opens into a guest bed; a red lacquered armoire holds linens. Most furnishings are designed by artists, including a coffee table by Gina Perlin and two-tiered shelf with drawers by Tim Rempel.*

*Photography by David Livingston*

**Left** *The small bedroom was kept nearly bare except for its major piece of sculpture — a bed of iron vines, by Eric Powell.*

**Below** *Dining-area walls are coated with pigmented plaster in an Italian ocher, creating a glow (with the help of a spotlight) despite a lack of windows nearby.*

**Opposite** *Living-room blinds, designed by Marc Melvin of canvas, muslin and other materials, are unfurled from the bottom up and filter light from the double-height windows. Notes of green in the furnishings echo the Robert Birmelin painting.*

**Above** *The galley kitchen's industrial-looking appliances imply that an old loft has been modernized. Abstract shoji doors, more webbed than gridded, were designed by Marc Melvin.*

# DAVID ROCKWELL & JAY M. HAVERSON

## A Classic in Miniature
New York City

700 square feet/65.03 square meters

On the gritty rooftop of a 1920s building, David Rockwell discovered an architect's dream: five abandoned maids' rooms orbiting a shared bath, all waiting to be gutted and rebuilt. The only restriction was the existing size, a total of 700 square feet.

Every aspect of Rockwell's new, one-bedroom home — designed with former architecture partner Jay M. Haverson — evokes a larger space. Eleven French doors lead to the terrace. The hearth is a reduced copy of a classical mantel. And the layout opens with an entry hall, which some architects, given the confines, might consider wasted space. "We planted a lot of visual clues," says Rockwell, "suggesting a scaled-down version of a larger home."

Many furnishings were eliminated in the blueprint stage. Bookshelves and cabinets, just ten inches wide, are notched into a short passage between the living room and bedroom. The architects also recessed a media cabinet in a living-room wall, concealing it behind a paneled door, and designed a niche just for Rockwell's electric piano. "I couldn't hide it," he says. "But I could stretch the apartment by building in as much as possible, and planning around the rest."

Left  *Street and rooftop views from the terrace add to the perceived space in every room.*

*Photography by Paul Warchol*

Above & Opposite  *The living room's tile floors are in sky colors; a tinge of peach in the walls cuts the contrast between indoors and out. A change of level between rooms enhances the sense of transition, suggesting a rambling apartment.*

**Left** *The bedroom is as economical with space as a ship's cabin, hence the porthole window. The bed's platform contains drawers and is flanked by built-in wardrobes; recessed shelves take the place of nightstands.*

**Below** *A double-coved ceiling and banks of windows magnify the tiny dining room. Because textures are called out — slate tabletop, webbed Shaker chairs, Brazilian mahogany floorboards — the setting could be kept spare.*

**Opposite** *The galley kitchen's great luxury, for New York, is a window over the sink. Glass cupboard-doors give the room depth; the contrast of clear and pebbled panes adds another layer of interest.*

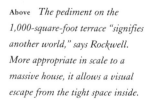

**Above** *The pediment on the 1,000-square-foot terrace "signifies another world," says Rockwell. More appropriate in scale to a massive house, it allows a visual escape from the tight space inside.*

# The Components of Calm

Washington, D.C.

1,080 square feet/100.33 square meters

**Opposite** *The living room's wall-to-wall curtains run straight to the corners to camouflage asymmetric windows. A wire lamp-base refrains from impeding a guest's line of sight.*

**Left** *The table in a dining corner is slipcovered for buffets; chairs face out, offering themselves as pull-up seating in the living room. The screen creates a slight enigma about the actual boundaries of the space.*

**Below** *Dixon expressed white in a multitude of textures, upholstering the living-room chairs in chenille, an ottoman by Vicente Wolf in leather, and the sofa in two hues of linen (the piping is lighter). The curve of a chair guides a visitor's gaze back to the center of the room.*

*Photography by Angie Seckinger*

When designer Barry Dixon focused the mirrors in this four-room apartment, he did so with the precision of a scientist aiming a laser beam. He leaned a tall, American Empire mirror against the wall so it caught an expanse of white ceiling, thus heightening the room. But he angled a 16th-century Venetian mirror down, framing a cloistered view of a seating area — and fostering intimacy.

The mirrors reflect a living room bathed in cream, from the striped silk curtains to the vast, tufted ottoman to the walls, painted to resemble pale stone. "The key to a small space," says Dixon, "is to dip it all in the same vat. I could have done every surface in charcoal, and it would seem just as large — because I would have employed all the same devices."

Within this luminous envelope are elements so diverse that a single tableskirt turns out to be made of easygoing linen, fullbodied silk, and hardware-store chain (75 cents a foot) draped at the corners. "The chain and the silk represent the extremes of how the room works, both formally and informally," says Dixon. "For lack of a bigger space, you need enough ambiguity to use the room both ways."

**Left** *To help the study double as a guest room, a flip-top writing table folds flat when the sofabed is pulled out. Pictures are matted in silver to reflect light; long tableskirts conceal out-of-season clothes; and a Federal style bulls eye mirror offers an expanded view of the room.*

**Below** *Dixon angled the owner's bed, focusing attention on the long diagonal in a confining bedroom. The headboard is a metal screen dragged out of an alleyway; paired with a Robert Rauschenberg painting, it draws the eye up.*

**Opposite** *Sofa pillows wear an overscaled* putti *print that provides a kind of visual narrative for the room, but they reverse to cream velvet when the guests are old-guard.*

# SANDRA NUNNERLEY

## Hard Edges, Soft Whites

New York City

900 square feet/83.61 square meters

Opposite  *When the daybed was angled into the library niche, the space visibly relaxed. Bookshelves were built ceiling-high and capped with molding, making them part of the architecture.*

*Photography by Paul Ryan*

Once Sandra Nunnerley had acquired the immeasurable river view, she had to deal with the white-box apartment that accompanied it. Bone structure could be installed, and character layered on. But how could three rooms accommodate her life?

To stretch her L-shaped living room, Nunnerley claimed the ell for a guest room and library; a down-filled daybed, canted out from a corner, sleeps one. Quiet strokes of luxury — like made-to-order Parisian fringe — make it hard to imagine that the owner could lack for space.

Because the front door opens into the living room, Nunnerley implied a foyer by positioning a table nearby. At night, set for dinner, it seats four or holds a buffet. Visitors, lulled by the rich serenity, never realize that one room is doing the job of five: entry hall, dining, living, guest quarters and book-lined study.

But the master stroke is a simple curtain — a river

of silk chiffon that falls from a curving track. That curve, says Nunnerley, was murder to engineer; but when the chiffon is swept into its arc, it prevails completely over the austere envelope of the room.

Above  *To enlarge the living room, Nunnerley contrasts various textures in a dozen shades of white: bleached wood floors, ivory walls, silk upholstery.*

Left  *Placement of the French Empire chandelier helps set the foyer-and-dining area apart from the rest of the living room. The raw-linen tableskirt is banded at the base with leather.*

Above  *When company arrives, a mix of chairs — some antique, some a stacking design by Philippe Starck — can be pulled up for dinner, or strewn about for a buffet.*

**Left** *Nunnerley designed the 12-foot sofa to accommodate large parties; a series of 18th-century Italian etchings hangs behind it, and a pair of Korean chests make an exotic coffee table. New crown moldings add detail and negate some of the bruising right angles.*

**Right** *Sumptuous materials, used sparingly, evoke old-world associations in a boxy bedroom. The stately Regency armoire, far more impressive than a bureau, conquers a low ceiling.*

**Below** *Subtle symmetry in the bedroom invites the eye to linger: A round frame is reiterated by the guéridon table; a Baccarat sconce is paired with its reflection. Nunnerley, designing the bed's knife-pleated covering and quilt, was inspired by Chanel couture.*

# GORALNICK ★ BUCHANAN

## A Timeless Interior
### New York City

1,000 square feet/92.9 square meters

When this old hospital building became an apartment house, it lost all traces of character. The designers confronted a white box with two bedrooms, no moldings, and one structural quirk — a thick column, oddly sited, and garishly clad in mirror.

But in this obstruction, Barry Goralnick and Michael Buchanan discovered the key to a more inviting layout. Rather than work around the column, they built three more — setting up a colonnade that flows past the living room toward the bedrooms. "The columns create circulation," Goralnick explains, "and by having to walk around them, you sense that the apartment is larger than it really is." They also removed a coat closet to create a small foyer, so that visitors were no longer deposited into the living room without a formal entry.

Next, an architectural sensibility was layered over the bare surfaces: The four columns are silhouetted like skyscrapers, with a banded, rooflike top. This articulation, reminiscent of detailing by Charles Rennie Mackintosh, grounds the interior in the past. The designers also installed picture-rail molding all the way around the room, which makes the ceiling appear higher than its eight-and-a-half feet. With its historic sensibility newly applied, the apartment gracefully declines to reveal its age.

**Left** *The newly created foyer is distinguished from the colonnade by its furnishings: a reproduction Empire chest and ornate Adamstyle mirror.*

**Below** *New floorboards run on the diagonal, making the colonnade appear wider. Columns were scored down the sides to make them appear more slender.*

*Photography by Dan Cornish*

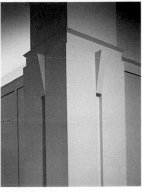

**Above** *For consistency in detailing, the band around the top of each column is the same height as the picture rail encircling the room. Paint colors — gray-white on top, dove gray below — are also identical.*

**Left** *Custom cabinetry adds storage space and separates the colonnade from the living room. To keep the two areas visually connected, however, parts of the divider are open on both sides, and a glass top adds translucency.*

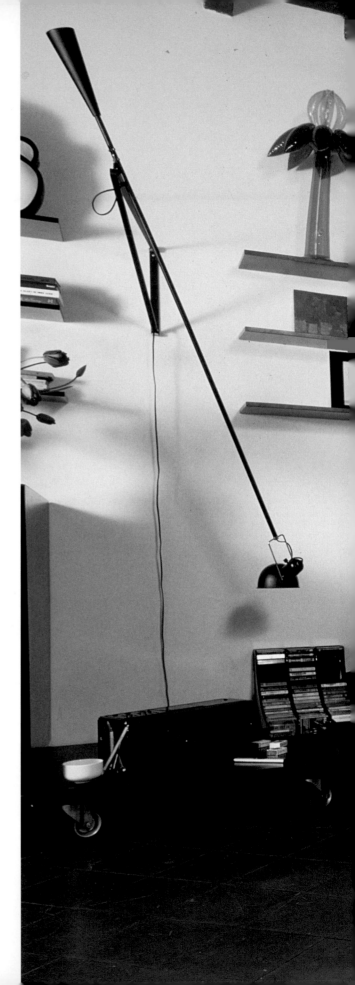

# TRANSIT DESIGN

## Enlarged by Art

Rome, Italy

540 square feet/50 square meters

To the late Nicolao Evaristo, an architect and collector, floorspace — not furniture — was the ultimate luxury. He edited down his possessions, dedicated his walls to unorthodox art, and designed furnishings he could literally push around. The result was half home and half gallery, more liberated than confined.

Many elements converged to expand these rooms. The paintings, for example, have a quality of dimension, so one's gaze is rarely stopped by the walls. Furnishings are distilled to Evaristo's idea of a minimum — a handful of chairs, which tend to migrate; a low sofa on steely casters; and a glass dining table mounted on a bicycle wheel so it can be rolled where it is needed. As for the white backdrop, it simply recedes behind the art.

"This is typical of his design," says Danilo Parisio, one of Transit's partners, all of whom collaborated on the interior. "He let the paintings expand the space."

Several other factors, inherited from history, work like a can-opener on this small apartment. Windows frame a complex landscape of red tile roofs. The wooden ceiling, crafted with the building in the early 1800s, runs through every room for a loftlike effect. With little furniture to interrupt the scene, a visitor's eye takes the measure of the space in a surprisingly grand sweep.

Above  *Furniture in the living room is treated graphically, with black shelves striping the walls. The pedestal for a thread-and-buttons sculpture by Claudio Cintolli opens into a bar.*

Right  *A low, black coffee table, when wheeled against the wall, joins with the sofa into a sleek and unobtrusive unit.*

*Photography by Janos Grapow*

Opposite *Evaristo entrusted his idea for the bicycle-wheeled dining table to a young sculptor, Mascello Blasi. Largely translucent, it commandeers little visual space.*

Left *The stack of books, a 19th-century metal piece, unfolds into library steps or serves as an end-table when closed.*

Left *The bed manages to look lithe — partly because it rests on a wafer of laminate, and partly because it wears colors taken from the art overhead, a 19th-century study of Pompeii.*

# GLENN GISSLER

## A Foyer's Largesse
### New York City

800 square feet/74.32 square meters

**Right** *In the dining area, a Philippe Starck table suits the contemporary architecture, while gilded 19th-century chairs ground the room in history.*

**Below** *Strong colors make the bedroom an extension of the living room; the overscaled headboard implies a sweeping space. Doors to the living room are actually front doors, chosen for stature; Gissler changed their clear panes to frosted glass.*

The problem, Glenn Gissler told his client, was not size, but gangly proportions. The front door opened smack into the living room, which in turn was long and narrow. With just two architectural strokes, however, Gissler gave this one-bedroom apartment its new rhythm.

He first constructed an entry vestibule, lowering its ceiling for intimacy. Now, instead of plunging into the living room, a visitor steps into a cool, gray-and-white transition space. "It's a decompression chamber," says Gissler. "Before you enter an apartment of strong colors and sparse, edited objects."

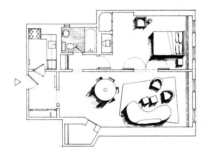

By slicing off space for an entry-way, he shortened the living room, correcting its tunnel-like dimensions. His second move was to break through the long wall between living room and bedroom. "By knocking open a double doorway," he says, "we gained a suite that was 22 feet across." The layout now invites wandering. It is furnished sculpturally, its sofa a biomorphic curve of red damask, its coffee table a burst of carving. A cascade of linen hides underscaled windows with security gates: "Long curtains are an important gesture," says Gissler. "They make this narrow room feel grander."

**Left & Below** *The living room, an unrelieved rectangle, is redeemed by asymmetry — furnishings set off-center on a five-sided rug. Rather than add moldings, Gissler hung Italian lighting fixtures to make a minimalist gallery of the walls.*

**Above** *The foyer holds a Tom Dixon chair made of metal scraps; its seat is a small manhole cover. Sinuous fabric, hung two feet in front of a plain wall, not only creates an instant closet but softens the hard-edged architecture.*

*Photography by Peter Margonelli*

# BRUCE BIERMAN

## A Place for Everything
New York City

1,100 square feet/102.19 square meters

Bruce Bierman comes home to an alley-narrow loft with a fire-escape view — and every element of luxury he could desire. First, for him, is the layering of white upon white: smooth plaster, crisp silk, the glow of ash floorboards. Second is visual serenity — not even a coffee cup intrudes on his sense of order.

This gentle precision is afforded by storage, elevated here to a high art. Bierman, who goes through life collecting few souvenirs, enlarges his home by filing away what he cannot live without. With an 11-foot-long dressing room slung with shelves and drawers, Bierman's bedroom is uncrowded by bureaus and therefore needs no walls to close it off. The result is an unimpeded, 50-foot view through the loft. "When your line of sight stays open," Bierman says, "you get a very expansive feeling."

A third luxury is that the loft transforms electronically into a personal theatre, making it more versatile than a space twice its size. With a corps of remote controls, Bierman can dim the lights, lower the blackout shades, summon down a 72-inch projection television screen, activate the sound system and roll a video. In a characteristic measure of orderliness, he then dispatches the controls to a mahogany box on the coffee table.

*A curtain of Italian silk sweeps between the living and sleeping areas for occasional privacy. Matched sets are rigorously avoided. The coffee table's copper top is wedded to steel cabriole legs from a Philippe Starck chair; and the mix of sofa, chaise and chair offers a multiplicity of choices in this 15-by-21-foot area.*

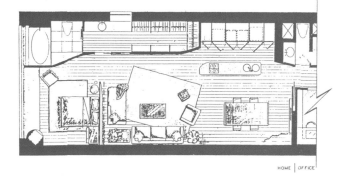

**Left**  *One-third of the 31-foot-long bath is devoted to clothing storage. Into this narrow zone, Bierman has squeezed 26 linear feet of hanging, nine linear feet of floor-to-ceiling shelving, and built-in stacks of drawers.*

**Below**  *Shower and sink are separated by a glass door, allowing daylight to spill across the length of the bath. To avoid strong contrasts that would visually shrink the space, Bierman designed a vanity of frosted and tinted glass.*

**Left** *The windowed end of the loft, delineated only by the low-slung headboard, holds the bed and little else. An entertainment column keeps the television from stealing floorspace.*

*Photography by Andrew Bordwin*

**Right & Above right** *Except for a granite island, sleek as an executive's desk, the kitchen can vanish behind floor-to-ceiling cabinet doors. With the cabinets open, appliances (including refrigerator and microwave) are revealed. At dinner parties, Bierman corrals dirty dishes behind the doors and instantly restores neatness to the loft.*

**Far right** *As insurance against disorder, kitchen storage drawers were designed to hold specific mugs and dishes.*

# CLODAGH

## A Working Retreat
New York City

500 square feet/46.45 square meters

Living in a penthouse can be like owning a slice of sky. But while a terrace extends this one-bedroom apartment, the interior has to double as a full-time office.

Karen Fisher, who lives and works here, owns Designer Previews, a national referral service that matches clients with interior designers. When her work began encroaching on every surface, Clodagh created an office in three cabinets that can be closed up every night. Two, used by Fisher and her assistant, are floor-to-ceiling stacks of shelves with pull-out desktops. A third conceals office machines, designers' portfolios and the odd kitchen platter. Cabinet doors are ceiling-high, colorwashed to match the walls and free of telltale knobs; and even the ceiling received

the same paint finish: "If you define the separation," explains Clodagh, "your eye starts worrying the transition."

But if the envelope is serene, the furnishings are rich: an antique Persian carpet, a 12-foot banquette, 19th-century Irish mahogany chairs. "A small space can look mean-spirited," says Clodagh, "without that touch of opulence."

**Above & Left**  *An assistant's work station rises nearly ten feet to the ceiling, but at 30 inches wide it makes minimal demands on floor-space. The open door across from it holds trays on a ledge and hides office storage when closed.*

**Opposite**  *For bedroom storage, cabinets rise like pillars on either side of the bed, becoming part of the architecture.*

*Photography by Andrew Garn*

Left   *A changing gallery in the living room includes "We have so much fun," an art piece by Joshua Neretin. Clodagh made the dining table from an old pedestal with a new, elliptical top of raw steel.*

Opposite   *A 12-foot banquette, designed by Clodagh, makes the living room seem not only welcoming but wider. The cushion is soft on one side and firm as a mattress on the other; it sleeps two, foot to foot. A ledge holds a rotating art display.*

# TRANSIT DESIGN

## When Storage Is Everything

Rome, Italy

540 square feet/50.17 square meters

The wedding-cake moldings of this apartment survived a major renovation when the building, once a monastery, went residential. The walls, however, bear no hint of the 19th century. Half of them, painted white, are backdrops for modern paintings. The other half are wrapped in blue-gray cabinetry — one architecture team's answer to the antique armoire.

The cabinets are lacquered with a fingerprint-resistant matte formula, normally used on metal. Their facade is comprised of panels, tall and flat, like plain pilasters. These panels glide on hidden rails to reveal books and collectibles, or swing back on hinges into the kitchen or bath, depending on where one is exploring. "Sometimes you find objects," says Danilo Parisio, a partner in Transit, "and other times you find doorways. The entire system is a kind of screen that draws the kitchen, bedroom, living room and bath into a unified space."

A kitchen doorway was relocated, and the space slightly enlarged. But the lacquered cabinetry acted as a kind of renovation without dust, bringing disparate rooms into a comprehensive whole and becoming the apartment's key piece of furniture. "With practical functions resolved by the cupboard system," explains the architect, "we could reduce the owner's furnishings to bare essentials."

**Right** *No visible hardware clutters the cabinets; metallic lacquered edges provide a touchpoint. By sliding the doors, the owner can reveal a different display every day.*

**Below** *With a wall of cabinetry facing the bed, the bedroom is freed of bureaus and other furnishings.*

*Photography by Janos Grapow*

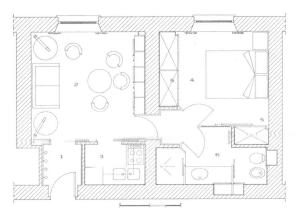

**Above**  *A sofabed in the living room accommodates guests; fluid curtains are a counterpoint to the cabinetry.*

**Left**  *A glass table by Alvar Aalto takes up little visual space; it serves as the sole dining area. Le Corbusier chairs, being round, offer comfort without bulk.*

# GIANFRANCO FRATTINI

## Privacy With Light
### Portofino, Italy

871.9 square feet/81 square meters

To give this apartment its sense of place, architect Gianfranco Frattini drew its tranquil colors from the landscape: an antique pink, from the weathered exteriors of Portofino's 15th-century houses, and sea-green, from the nearby gulf.

But he also gave the two-bedroom flat the sensibility of a loft, with rooms delineated by partial walls. "I aspired to a feeling of 'oneness,' of a single volume made up of smaller spaces," Frattini says. He also wanted to ensure that daylight, entering through windows at the long ends of this narrow apartment, could reach the dark interior.

Frattini's key partition is an engineering feat: A shelving unit about six feet high, it conceals a gridded panel that glides to the ceiling at the press of a button. The result is privacy without light deprivation. "Because the grid is not solid," says Frattini, "you don't feel boxed in when it's up." The base of the shelving, a hinged flap, conceals two low, wheeled beds that pull out into the living room for guests. In the morning, they are garaged under a raised floor of the adjacent master bedroom.

The apartment has a spare esthetic, with its tailored upholstery and bare tile floors. But when sunlight spreads over the pink walls, it creates a backdrop as luminous and atmospheric as the Portofino air.

*Living-room windows wear white cotton blinds that filter sunlight. A floor of white ceramic tile was laid throughout, bolstering the impression that the space is merely zoned, not divided into rooms.*

Opposite  *The bedroom's green-varnished wood and pink walls, carried over from the living room, create continuity. Frattini elevated its floor so that guest-beds could be stowed underneath; they slide out on the living-room side of the partition.*

Left & Below  *Even with its gridded panel retracted, the shelving unit in the living room shields the owner's bed from view. Shelves are lacquered dark blue, a reference to the sea. A system of dimmers allows different zones to be darkened or lit by recessed halogen bulbs.*

Above  *From the businesslike foyer, a visitor can turn left into the dining and living area, or follow several steps toward the bath and a hall lined with closets.*

*Photography by
Giuseppe Molteni/Roberta Motta*

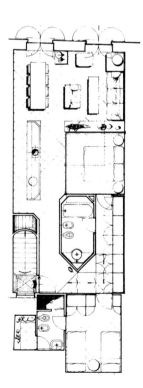

# SOUTH BEACH DESIGN

## A Studio Divided
Miami Beach, Florida

575 square feet/53.42 square meters

Some rooms do not submit easily to surgery. This was one: While its designers prescribed separate zones for sleeping and entertaining, they did not want to corrupt the 1920s proportions with a divisive, full-height wall.

Instead, design partners Barrie Livingstone and Chris Raessler built a sweeping curve of glass block. Two feet short of the ceiling, it delineates the bedroom area, admits light, and even cre-

ates a formal entryway to one side. The interior now unfolds as a visitor enters, rather than revealing itself all at once.

Because the client lives with dark antiques, the designers kept everything else light and spare. They aged the walls in a parchment finish. They merely hinted at drapery, with a swag held high by gilded gargoyles. And they designed the two-piece sofa, with its traditional profile, to precisely fit its corner: "A regular sofa would leave gaps on each side, which would shrink the space," says Livingstone. Finally, using only a paintbrush, they heightened the art deco pilasters — marbleizing up past their tops and straight to the ceiling. Explains Livingstone: "It lifts the whole room."

**Above** *The designers used a 300-year-old English mirror to bounce light and interior views around, but never succumbed to that Miami cliché, the mirrored wall.*

**Right** *In the living room, a narrow wedge of wall gains prominence with a strapping arrangement of prints and maps.*

*Photography by Carlos Baez*

**Above** *An iron bed in the French campaign style practically fills the space. But its frame is not solid, and the antique French nightstands are unusually narrow; as a result, the bed does not consume the room.*

**Left** *In a bedroom niche just 17 inches deep, the designers built a mahogany-stained maple cabinet that eliminates the need for a bureau. The curtain, when open, takes up less space than a door.*

# GORALNICK ★ BUCHANAN

## Enriching the Backdrop
New York City

650 square feet/60.4 square meters

The client suffered from what architect Barry Goralnick calls "the New York problem" — too many books, too little storage, a slender budget, and a one-bedroom rental apartment that could be redecorated but not remodeled.

Goralnick and his partner, designer Michael Buchanan, addressed all four issues with a single, expansive gesture: an 18-foot shelving unit that runs, floor-to-ceiling, the length of the living room. Paintings and old photographs hang on the shelves, as if the walls alone could not contain them, and the resulting layers of books and art give the apartment depth. So do the substantial crown molding and baseboard, additions that encircle the room and give the shelves their stature. "It's a trick of the eye," says Goralnick, " but overscaled moldings make you experience a small space as larger."

The bedroom was so small and dark that the partners, unable to air it out, evoked instead the dense, opulent interior of a Fabergé egg. The walls of this 10-by-12-foot cubicle are painted Russian blue — a shade they had computer-matched to a piece of 18th-century pottery — and trimmed with a wallpaper border that resembles a gilded crown molding. "The window treatments are heavy; the walls are vibrant," says Buchanan. "It goes against a lot of the rules for a small space, but it makes the room a jewel."

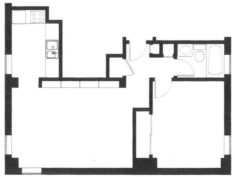

**Above** *Goralnick and Buchanan overscaled the key objects in the living room, upholstering the 19th-century sofa with a broad stripe and unfurling an Empire-style rug. Orion sconces are their own design.*

*Photography by Gary Rogers*

**Above** *Touches of gold — from the picture frames to the coffee table legs — unite disparate styles in the living room. Curtains, artworks and books are carried to the crown molding, creating a uniform impression of height.*

**Far left** *Furnishings in front of the wall of books add another layer to this detailed backdrop. The inlaid Harlequin table is a Goralnick ★ Buchanan design.*

**Left** *The far end of the living room was left spare to delineate the dining area, a spot distinguished by the room's only chandelier and several key omissions: rugs, heavy draperies, and table lamps.*

159

**Above** *The kitchen's harvest-gold appliances could not be disguised, but they receded after walls were painted a warmer yellow. The blue ceiling, covered in handprinted paper, draws the eye up and adds dimension to a narrow space.*

**Above** *To transform an ordinary bath, the designers papered the walls and ceiling in old-world red, installed a gilded crown molding, and treated the room as a tiny gallery. A visitor barely notices the mass-produced tiles.*

**Below & Right** *The bedroom's sole window is draped to imply architectural significance; and gold, applied liberally in the form of frames, fabrics and trimmings, turns an impossibly small room into a rich retreat.*

# CARL D'AQUINO & PAUL LAIRD

## A Majestic Maisonette
### New York City

875 square feet/81.3 square meters

In the basement of an apartment building, designer Carl D'Aquino and architect Paul Laird gutted a cluster of storage rooms. There, in that windowless space, they crafted a library so rich that it generates its own shimmer. Its walls are lined in honey-colored Karelian birch, and moldings are carved from walnut. A band of 22-karat gold leaf races just under the ceiling. "It's a jewel box," D'Aquino says. "A very small one."

The library is the lower level of a one-bedroom maisonette, that rare New York apartment that lies within a large building but has a private door to the street. Its one-room upper level serves as a suite: salon, breakfast area and master bedroom, divided not by walls but by an architectural unit of lacquer, glass and gold leaf. The basement, added later, is so narrow that Laird contrived an illusion: He curved one of the paneled walls, making the room appear longer, and built circular, glassed-in "rooms" at either end. (One is a foyer, the other a bar.) The preponderance of glass is more effective than an acre of windows. "You cannot conceive how small it is," says Laird. "It's an exquisite bit of trickery."

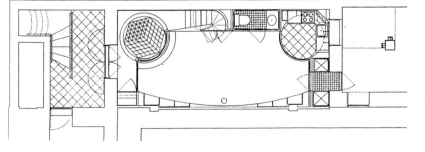

**Above** *A structural column rudely interrupted the library — until, sheathed in Karelian birch, it became a defining centerpiece.*

**Opposite** *D'Aquino chose library furnishings with varied pedigrees, but one sensibility: all are opulent, curvaceous and underscaled. The art deco divan was designed for the* Normandie *by Jules Leleu; the gold-winged Tuscan chair is a century older.*

*Photography by George Mott, Paul Warchol & Oberto Gili*

Far left  *Downstairs, at one end of the library, a round entrance court is set off by a curved and sliding door. Floor-to-ceiling glass creates an interior window — much needed in a room whose sole opening is a front door below street level.*

Left  *The entrance court is so compressed that the library, just beyond, appears generous. Between the rich woods and complex fenestration, a visitor may wonder if he has stepped into an heirloom cabinet rather than a tiny foyer.*

Above  *Upstairs, the kitchenette, set into one side of a lacquered room divider, was designed to double as a bar. The stairs lead discreetly to the bedroom loft.*

Left  *Chairs by Charles Rennie Mackintosh, with an oval aluminum table by Laird, bestow dining-room stature on an angular sliver of space. A sandblasted rear window admits only light.*

Opposite  *Gold leaf is the salon's major source of indirect lighting; D'Aquino used it to line a niche designed for artworks, applied it to his own demi-lune table, and sought it in antiques. An over-scaled crown molding keeps a high ceiling from appearing remote.*

# BARBARA SOUTHERLAND

## A Working Pied-a-Terre
New York City

488 square feet/45.34 square meters

When clients come to this terraced and restful living room, they assume that the rest of the apartment is simply off limits. In fact, they're seeing it all: bedroom (a pull-out sofa), dining room (a gray-skirted table) and office (the same multipurpose table).

What visitors don't see are the tricks and techniques that give this studio its flexibility. The loveseat, for example, seems too lithe to be a sofabed. A portable television hides behind an armchair, though at night it gets lifted onto the wheeled "whatnot" and rolled into view. For a guest room, a leopard-print ottoman unfolds into a studio bed. And a separate dressing area houses built-in storage, so there are no telltale bureaus to reveal the room's double life.

The round table, in particular, plays many roles. Forty inches across, it accommodates client conferences, sketching and other design work, as well as meals. Its base, a shelved cupboard, is a secret storage site. Southerland conceals her books in a closet, reserving shelves around the fireplace for display.

Two extra pockets of space make this studio feel almost generous: the foyer, which implies that a larger spread of rooms lies beyond, and the terrace, which holds a table for two. Southerland keeps it planted with palm trees and begonias, and uses it as a bar during parties; it serves as a bonus room three seasons out of four.

**Above** *Though intimate enough for dinner, this silk-skirted table is lamp-lit and glass-topped for client meetings. Striped Roman blinds keep the studio tailored.*

**Left** *The terrace's railing allows one's view to travel far past the apartment, offering visual relief from its confines. The cafe table is suitably scaled to the eight-foot-deep space.*

*Photography by Alec Hemer*

*Pressed tropical leaves create a statuesque arrangement when identically framed and massed. Nesting tables, at right, can be pulled out as needed for paperwork or drinks.*

**Above** *A butler's tray table in the foyer keeps keys, mail and gloves from encroaching on the single room beyond. The Hitchcock chairs migrate into the living room when needed for company.*

**Left** *Two mismatched easy chairs became a pair when dressed in the same Rose Cummings chintz. The rug is linen and cotton: "It feels like corduroy," says Southerland, "and being light, it enlarges the room."*

# GREG JORDAN

## The Urban Envelope
### New York City

500 square feet/46.45 square meters

When a man collects books and prints, surrounds himself with lustrous antiques and tends to stockpile magazines, it helps if he does not also live in a three-room apartment. Rather than move, however, designer Greg Jordan wrapped his rooms and half his furnishings in a single print until the boundaries all but melted.

The print, upon close examination, is chain-link fencing—or what Jordan, who designed it, calls "the urban version of 19th-century English trellis." Because the links are diagonal they seem to expand, much as a checkerboard floor painted on the diagonal will visually widen a room. "It really does push the walls out," says Jordan. A white ground establishes the print as a neutral, and against this urban-trellis backdrop, the life of the living room—its books and paintings, ceramics and flowers, even the flash of blue from a silk lampshade—appears in sharp relief.

Jordan knew that if the chain link was to recede, rather than advance on the space, it would have to envelope all of his overscaled seating—wing chairs, arm chairs, sofa, ottoman, even a clever banquette near the hearth that is almost indistinguishable from the wall behind it. "Everything soft becomes a single element," he says. "If it hadn't, the apartment would seem even smaller than it is."

*Left  Steel-gray cotton lines the chain-link bedcurtains, creating a sense of architecture that defines the height and breadth of the bed. Continuity in the details, like a blue silk lampshade whose mate is in the living room, helps unify a small and segmented apartment.*

*Above  Furnishings not wrapped in chain-link fabric are, instead, nearly transparent—like the glass-and-metal coffee table, and bamboo bookshelves with no solid sides. Painting by Jerry Whitworth.*

*Photography by Alec Hemer*

*Opposite  Jordan designed his own Hepplewhite chairs with deep seating and extra curves, then relegated them to the backdrop by painting their frames white. The Batman mirror is his update on a 19th-century English design.*

# DIRECTORY

**Ace Architects**
Lucia Howard
David Weingarten
300 Second Street, No.1
Oakland, California 94607
Tel: (510) 452-0775
Fax: (510) 452-1175

**Bierly-Drake Associates, Inc.**
Lee Bierly
Christopher Drake
17 Arlington Street
Boston, Massachusetts 02116
Tel: (617) 247-0081
Fax: (617) 247-6395

**Bruce Bierman**
**Bruce Bierman Design, Inc.**
29 West 15th Street
New York, New York 10011
Tel: (212) 243-1935
Fax: (212) 243-6615

**Brad Blair**
**Charles Jacobsen, Inc.**
8687 Melrose Avenue
West Hollywood, California 90069
Tel: (310) 652-1188
Fax: (310) 652-2555

**Agnes Bourne, Inc.**
2 Henry Adams Square, No.220
San Francisco, California 94103
Tel: (415) 626-6883
Fax: (415) 626-2489

**Gregory D. Cann**
**Cann + Company**
529 Main Street, Suite 204
Boston, Massachusetts 02129
Tel: (617) 338-8814
Fax: (617) 338-7337

**Clodagh Design International**
Clodagh
Robert Pierpont
365 First Avenue
New York, New York 10010
Tel: (212) 673-9202
Fax: (212) 614-9125

**Carl D'Aquino**
**Carl D'Aquino Interiors, Inc.**
180 Varick Street
New York, New York 10014
Tel: (212) 929-9787
Fax: (212) 929-9225

**Barry Dixon**
**Barry Dixon, Inc.**
2019 Q Street, N.W.
Washington, DC 20008
Tel: (202) 332-7955
Fax: (202) 332-7952

**Mary Douglas Drysdale**
**Drysdale Design Associates**
1733 Connecticut Avenue, N.W.
Washington, DC 20009
Tel: (202) 588-0700
Fax: (202) 588-5086

**Gianfranco Frattini**
**Gianfranco Frattini, Architect**
Via S. Agnese 14
Milan, Italy
Tel: 02 856585
Fax: 02 72027703

**Doree Friedman**
**Fine Line Construction**
1715 Ninth Street
Berkeley, California 94710
Tel: (510) 524-1444
Fax: (510) 524-1492

**Glenn Gissler**
**Glenn Gissler Design, Inc.**
174 Fifth Avenue, No.402
New York, New York 10010
Tel: (212) 727-3220
Fax: (212) 727-3225

**Goodman Charlton, Inc.**
Jeffrey Goodman
Steven Charlton
1500 Rising Glen Road
Los Angeles, California 90069
Tel: (310) 657-7068
Fax: (310) 657-1868

**Goralnick ★ Buchanan**
**A&D Inc.**
Barry Goralnick
Michael Buchanan
306 East 61st Street
New York, New York 10021
Tel: (212) 644-0334
Fax: (212) 644-0904

**Jay M. Haverson**
**Haverson Architecture &**
**Design**
289 Greenwich Avenue
Greenwich, Connecticut 06830
Tel: (203) 629-8300
Fax: (203) 629-8399

**Greg Jordan**
**Greg Jordan, Inc.**
504 East 74th Street, Suite 4W
New York, New York 10021
Tel: (212) 570-4470
Fax: (212) 570-6660

**Paul Laird**
**Paul Laird, Architect**
458 Maple Street
Litchfield, Connecticut 06759
Tel: (203) 567-0265

**W. Jude LeBlanc**
**W. Jude LeBlanc, Architect**
881 Massachusetts Avenue
Cambridge, Massachusetts 02139
Tel: (617) 491-8064

**MacNelly • Cohen Architects**
Linda Joy Cohen
Bruce MacNelly
Post Office Box 2298
Vineyard Haven
Massachusetts 02568
Tel/Fax: (508) 693-4043

**Galal Mahmoud**
**Galal Mahmoud, Architect**
24, rue Vieille du Temple
75004 Paris, France
Tel: 48 87 07 08
Fax: 42 77 01 81

**Donald Maxcy Design**
**Associates**
Donald L. Maxcy
Marsha Maxcy
The Union Icehouse
600 East Franklin Street
Monterey, California 93940
Tel: (408) 649-6582
Fax: (408) 649-0519

**Marc Melvin**
**Marc Melvin Design**
3455 Filmore Street, Suite 304
San Francisco, California 94123
Tel: (415) 567-1484

**Sandra Nunnerley**
**Sandra Nunnerley, Inc.**
112 East 71st Street
New York, New York 10021
Tel: (212) 472-9341
Fax: (212) 472-9346

**Carol Olten**
**Carol Olten Design**
7245 Eads Avenue
La Jolla, California 92037
Tel: (619) 454-3660

**Richar**
**Richar Interiors, Inc.**
833 North Orleans Street,
Suite 3C
Chicago, Illinois 60610
Tel: (312) 951-0924
Fax: (312) 951-8535

**David Rockwell**
**Rockwell Architecture,**
**Planning & Design**
5 Union Square West
New York, New York 10003
Tel: (212) 463-0334
Fax: (212) 463-0335

**The South Beach Design**
**Group**
Barrie Livingstone
Chris Raessler
420 Lincoln Road, Suite 385
Miami Beach, Florida 33139
Tel: (305) 672-8800
Fax: (305) 672-9966

**Barbara Southerland**
**Barbara Southerland Inc.**
**Interior Decoration & Design**
Post Office Box 3474
Greenville
North Carolina 27836-1474
Tel: (919) 830-1020
Fax: (919) 830-1444

**Richard Stacy**
**Tanner Leddy Maytum Stacy**
444 Spear Street
San Francisco, California 94105
Tel: (415) 394-5400
Fax: (415) 394-8400

**Stamps & Stamps**
Kate Stamps
Odom Stamps
517 South Burnside Avenue
Los Angeles, California 90036
Tel: (213) 933-5698
Fax: (213) 930-0065

**Guy Stansfeld**
**Guy Stansfeld Architects**
359 Portobello Road
London W10 5SA, England
Tel: 081 964 0999
Fax: 081 960 9094

**Diane Thompson**
**Modern Living**
8125 Melrose Avenue
Los Angeles, California 90046
Tel: (213) 655-3898
Fax: (213) 655-1677

**Transit Design**
Giovanni Ascarelli
Maurizio Macciocchi
Danilo Parisio
Via Emilio Morosini, 17
00153 Rome, Italy
Tel: 06 5899848
Fax: 06 5898431

**Eric Watson**
**Eric Watson, Architect**
Post Office Box 4605
Seaside, Florida 32459-4605
Tel: (904) 231-4541
Fax: (904) 231-2720

**Carlos Baez**
**Carlos Baez Photographer**
8625 S.W. 43rd Street
Miami, Florida 33155
Tel: (305) 221-0125
Fax: (305) 795-6992

**Andrew Bordwin**
70A Greenwich Avenue, No.332
New York, New York 10011
Tel: (212) 633-0382
Fax: (212) 633-1046

**Beatriz Coll**
**Coll Photography**
2415 3rd Street, Suite 265
San Francisco, California 94107
Tel: (415) 863-0699
Fax: (415) 861-4582

**Dan Cornish**
38 Evergreen Road
New Canaan, Connecticut 06840
Tel: (203) 972-3714

**Jean-Etienne Fortunier**
79 rue de L'eglise
Paris 75015, France
Tel: 44 26 38 47

**Jack Gardner**
**Jack Gardner Photography, Inc.**
P.O. Box 7
Valparaiso, Florida 32580
Tel: (904) 678-7702

**Andrew Garn**
85 East 10th Street
New York, New York 10003
Tel: (212) 353-8434

**Russ Gilbert**
**Gilbert Photography**
13279 Saddle Ridge
Lakeside, California 92040
Tel: (619) 443-7769

**Oberto Gili**
31 West 11th Street
New York, New York 10011
Tel: (212) 255-7293

**David Glomb**
**David Glomb Photography**
458 ½ N. Genesee Avenue
Los Angeles, California 90036
Tel: (213) 655-4491
Fax: (212) 651 1437

**Janos Grapow**
Via Monti Parioli 49/0
Roma, Italy
Tel: 06 3244381

**Sam Gray**
**Sam Gray Photography**
409 West Broadway
South Boston
Massachusetts 02127
Tel: (617) 268-3933

**Alec Hemer**
626 East 20th Street
New York, New York 10009
Tel: (212) 982-5090

**Thibault Jeanson**
425 West 23rd Street
New York, New York 10011
Tel: (212) 243-2750

**José King**
**José King Photography**
30, Base Flat A
Cumberland Street
London SW1V 1LX, England
Tel: 071 630 7381
Fax: 081 960 9094

**Andy Lautman**
**Lautman Photography**
4906 41st Street, N.W.
Washington, DC 20016
Tel: (202) 966-2800

**David Livingston**
1036 Erica Road
Mill Valley, California 94941
Tel: (415) 383-0898
Fax: (415) 383-0897

**David Lund**
**Lund Photography**
2718 Stetson Lane
Houston, Texas 77043
Tel: (713) 690-6453
Fax: (713) 690-0052

**Peter Margonelli**
524 Broadway
New York, New York 10012
Tel: (212) 941-0380

**Pietro Mari**
Via Monti Si Biuini 24
Roma, Italy
Tel: 06 87190014

**Giuseppe Molteni**
Piazza S. Eustorgio 4
Milano, Italy
Tel: 02 8360209

**George Mott**
51 Bank Street
New York, New York 10014
Tel: (212) 242-2753

**Roberta Motta**
Piazza S. Eustorgio 4
Milano, Italy
Tel: 02 8360209

**Gary Rogers**
**Schoner Wohnen**
Papenhuder Strasse 49
Hamburg, Germany
Tel: 49-40-229 86 74

**Eric Roth**
**Eric Roth Studio**
337 Summer Street
Boston, Massachusetts 02210
Tel: (617) 338-5358
Fax: (617) 338-6098

**Paul Ryan**
27 Lytton Avenue
Palmers Green
London N134EH, England

**Angie Seckinger**
**Angie Seckinger Photography**
11231 Bybee Street
Silver Spring, Maryland 20902
Tel: (301) 649-3183
Fax: (301) 649-5830

**Robert Schellhammer**
**Our House Photography**
P.O. Box 4085
Vineyard Haven
Massachusetts 02568
Tel: (508) 693-8271
Fax: (508) 693-4826

**Tim Street-Porter**
2074 Watsonia Terrace
Los Angeles, California 90068
Tel: (213) 874-4278

**Dominique Vorillon**
1636 Silverwood Terrace
Los Angeles, California 90026
Tel: (213) 660-5883

**Paul Warchol**
133 Mulberry Street, No.6S
New York, New York 10013
Tel: (212) 431-3461
Fax: (212) 247-1953

**Alan Weintraub**
2325 3rd Street, No.325A
San Francisco, California 94107
Tel: (415) 553-8191
Fax: (415) 553-8192

**James Yochum**
12330 Betty May
Sawyer, Michigan 49125
Tel: (616) 426-8484
Fax: (616) 426-8485

**Marco P. Zecchin**
**Image Center**
1219 Willow Mar Drive
San Jose, California 95118
Tel: (408) 723-3649

# INDEX

# Acknowledgments

Many people contributed generously to this book. I am grateful, first, to the photographers, designers and architects who allowed me to feature their work...to Donna Warner, Editor in Chief of *Metropolitan Home* magazine, for writing the foreword and for being a source of inspiration and support...to Dominick Abel, my agent, for his expertise and sound advice...and to Rima Suqi, whose research helped give this book its international scope.

Many editors, designers and publicists opened their Rolodexes to me — a critical contribution. I am particularly indebted to the following:

*Metropolitan Home* magazine — specifically Arlene Hirst, senior editor, design news; and city editors Donna Paul, Lisa Skolnik, Nisi Berryman, Lisa Cicotte and Ruth Reiter

Designer Previews: Karen Fisher (New York) and Michael Walsh (Chicago)

Mike Strohl, Design Media Resource

Steven Wagner, Editor in Chief, Hachette Filipacchi New Media

Tim Street-Porter, photographer and author

Christopher Hirsheimer, *Saveur* and *Garden Design* magazines

Rhoda Jaffin Murphy, contributing editor, *American HomeStyle & Gardening* magazine

Betty J. Rossbach, Seaside

And the following interior designers: Glenn Gissler, Annie Kelly, Juan Menendez, BJ Peterson, Paul Siskin and Marshall Watson

The entire staff of PBC International was deeply involved in shaping this book. For brevity, let me thank four: Susan Kapsis, managing editor; Richard Liu, technical director; Dorene Evans, project coordinator; and the designer, Garrett Schuh.